Prosperity Plans

How to create a low-cost small home that can grow over time.

New house and old house. Wolf Creek Farms, Georgia, photo by Arthur Rothstein, 1935
See Design 6515

A complete reprint of the 1935 booklet, *Farmhouse Plans*, by the U.S. Department of Agriculture, with forty small house designs, in a twenty-first century edition with Internet sources of working drawings and construction details

Edited by Donald J. Berg, AIA

www.ProsperityPlans.net

Contents:

Farmhouse Plans

Cover Sheet, Credits and Pages 1-70 from the 1935 book, *Farmhouse Plans* (USDA Farmers' Bulletin # 1738)

Farm family, on U.S. 64, eastern Oklahoma, photo by Dorethea Lange, 1938

Forward

By the time that the U.S. stock market crashed in 1929, signaling the start of the Great Depression, most farmers had already been suffering hard times for years. Plummeting produce prices and increasing competition from big, industrialized farms made it difficult for many small farm families to get by.

To make ends meet, family farmers tried to expand their production by buying more land and by investing in expensive machinery. They financed the costs by loans on their farmstead buildings and land.

Widespread droughts and even lower produce prices in the early 1930s meant that many farmers could not repay those loans. Hundreds of thousands of families lost their homes and land to foreclosures and farmstead auctions. Hundreds of thousands of other families tried to hold on, using any available money to pay the interest on their loans and in desperate attempts to increase production. Homes were poorly maintained and rarely modernized. Photographs from back then show the countryside full of dilapidated houses and impoverished people.

IV

Sharecropper family, photo by Dorethea Lange, 1937

Starting in 1933, as part of Franklin Roosevelt's New Deal, the United States government put a great number of men and women to work on projects to help farmers improve their living conditions. New rural roads and electrification projects like the Tennessee Valley Authority got most of the funding and publicity, but there were smaller projects that helped too.

The U.S. Department of Agriculture provided funds to agricultural colleges across the country to hire out-of-work engineers and architects. They were put to use preparing efficient farm building plans and instructional booklets on farmstead water supply, sanitation, lighting and heating.

The booklets and the construction plans were offered at prices that farmers could afford. Most of the booklets cost just ten cents each and the plans sold for just enough to cover the cost of printing.

The first plans were for inexpensive houses that could replace the run-down shacks and cabins that were homes to many families. They were small and simple to build. Farmers were encouraged to save cost by doing some of the construction and finish work themselves and by building with stone and wood from their own land.

Photo taken between 1935 and 1942

The little houses were designed to be sturdy, safe and much more convenient than the shacks that they replaced. Indoor bathrooms, not common at the time in most rural areas, were planned for all but the tiniest homes. Many planned on central heating and other modern conveniences like refrigerators and built-in cabinets.

The floor plans were perfect for working farm families. The new amenities were simply added to all of the common-sense features of traditional American farmhouses.

Kitchens were the most important rooms. They were always the center of farmhouses and of farms. Their windows looked out to barnyards and to roads so that farm women could keep an eye on things. Kitchens served the family, but were also harvest-time factories for any of the farm's products that had to be cooked, canned, or preserved. Kitchen porches, back porches, workrooms and root cellars extended the work and storage areas. Back or side doors, near kitchens, were the main entrances.

The homes had first floor bedrooms, not far from the kitchens, for use as sick rooms or nurseries. Living rooms and dining rooms, if included, were secondary spaces. Dining tables were often placed in the kitchen. Living rooms were sometimes just flexible spaces that also served as bedrooms.

The homes were designed in a variety of styles. Most were simplified versions of popular Colonial Revival styles, but some were daring, flat roofed "modernistic" homes. There were some vernacular designs like log cabins and southwestern adobe houses.

House at Magnolia Homesteads, Mississippi, photo by Arthur Rothstein, 1936
See Design 6521

Forty of the best designs were presented in the booklet that you'll find reproduced in this new book, the USDA Farmers' Bulletin No. 1738, *Farmhouse Plans*.

As you'll see, the booklet itself wasn't very different from many home plan catalogs that were popular at the time, and really not that different from house plan magazines and Internet websites that we have today. The designs were each presented with a full description of their features, floor plans, a pretty rendering of the farmhouse and a catalog number that people could use to order the plans.

But, Farmers' Bulletin No. 1738 sold for ten cents when most home plan catalogs were selling for a dollar or two. It presented attractive, solid little houses that worked well for farm families and that were inexpensive to build. It offered good quality blueprints for nothing but the cost of printing and postage.

And, it offered much more.

In the depths of the Great Depression, when drought and poverty devastated the countryside, when wind-blown, dust bowl dirt was dropping on their drafting tables, a group of engineers and architects somehow put despair aside. Instead of designing cheap small houses that were appropriate for the times that they were in, they created for the future that might be. They created plans for prosperity.

Most of the designs are of what the booklet calls "Growing Houses." They are fascinating homes that were carefully planned to be built in two or three stages. They were meant to expand from tiny dwellings into fairly gracious farmhouses that were homes, in the words of the booklet, "of dignity and charm."

The Growing Houses could be expanded in logical progressions with very little disruption to the previously built sections. Closets would become halls. Windows would be replaced with doors to new rooms. Kitchens, fireplaces, chimneys, staircases and living spaces would have very few alterations so that family life wouldn't be affected by the new construction.

Homesteader laying brick walk. Penderlea Homesteads, North Carolina, photo by Carl Mydans, 1936

Since the most effective way to cut construction cost has always been to build as small a structure as possible, Growing Houses were the perfect designs for their times. First stage, core houses of as little as 490 square feet could serve the needs of small families and could be built on a very limited budget. Additions could be built as necessary and as times got better.

For families confined to a cramped house, the idea that it was just the first step toward something better must have been inspiring. Renderings and floor plans of completed Growing Houses from the booklet would probably be produced to show relatives and neighbors what to expect. Some of the same drawings probably made it into frames over the mantels in some of the little homes.

After most of a decade of grueling years of horrible, horrible times, the underemployed engineers who created the Growing Houses and the farmers who built them were able to share the idea that prosperity was in their future and that, little by little, they could build towards it.

They were right.

House and garage at Magnolia Homesteads, Lauderdale County, Mississippi, photo by Arthur Rothstein, 1935   See Design 6514

About the Reprint

The following pages are direct reprints from Farmers' Bulletin #1738, *Farmhouse Plans*, by Wallace Ashby, published by the United States Department of Agriculture in 1935. The inside front cover, credits and pages one through seventy of that booklet follow this page.

U. S. DEPARTMENT OF AGRICULTURE

FARMERS' BULLETIN No. 1738

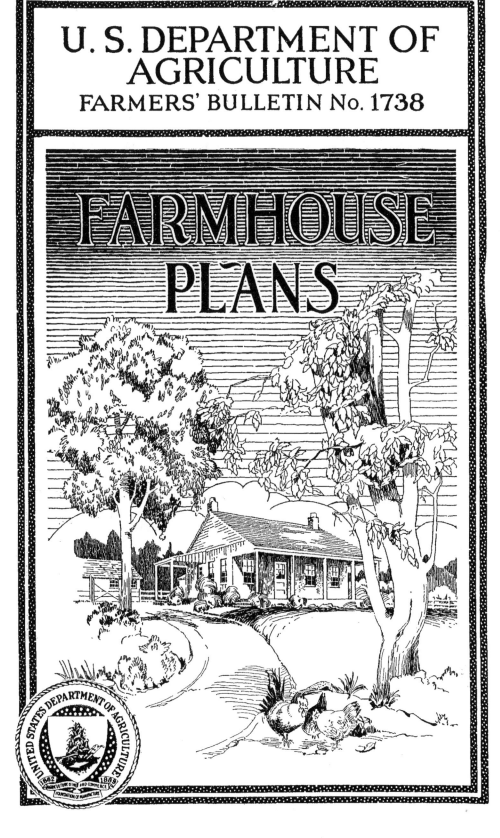

FARMHOUSE PLANS

THE FARMHOUSE PLANS presented in this bulletin were developed in connection with the Farm Housing Survey made in the spring of 1934 by the United States Department of Agriculture and the agricultural colleges of 46 States, with funds provided by the Civil Works Administration. These plans were selected from more than 100 prepared under the cooperation of the following agencies and persons:

United States Department of Agriculture: Bureau of Agricultural Engineering, S. H. McCrory, Chief; Bureau of Home Economics, Louise Stanley, Chief, and Director of the Rural Housing Survey.

Alabama Polytechnic Institute: J. B. Wilson, extension engineer, department of agricultural engineering.

University of Arkansas: Deane G. Carter, head, department of agricultural engineering.

University of California: H. B. Walker, head, division of agricultural engineering.

University of Georgia: R. H. Driftmier, professor of agricultural engineering.

University of Illinois: E. W. Lehmann, head, and W. A. Foster, assistant chief in rural architecture, department of agricultural engineering.

Purdue University (Indiana): William Aitkenhead, head, department of agricultural engineering.

Iowa State College: Henry Giese, professor, department of agricultural engineering.

Kansas State Agricultural College: H. E. Wichers, rural architect, department of architecture.

Massachusetts Agricultural College: C. I. Gunness, head, department of agricultural engineering.

University of Minnesota: H. B. White, assistant professor, division of agricultural engineering.

University of Missouri: J. C. Wooley, chairman, department of agricultural engineering.

Ohio State University: R. C. Miller, professor, department of agricultural engineering.

Agricultural and Mechanical College of Texas: D. Scoates, head, department of agricultural engineering.

Virginia Polytechnic Institute: C. E. Seitz, head, department of agricultural engineering.

State College of Washington: L. J. Smith, head, department of agricultural engineering.

University of Wisconsin: S. A. Witzel, extension instructor, department of agricultural engineering.

At each of the cooperating institutions, home economics specialists were consulted by the designers in regard to the arrangement of the kitchen and other parts of the home.

Working drawings for building the houses shown in this bulletin are available from the extension services of the State agricultural colleges. In most cases a small charge is made for the drawings.

Washington, D.C.

Issued October 1934
Slightly revised March 1935

FARMHOUSE PLANS

By WALLACE ASHBY, *Chief, Division of Structures, Bureau of Agricultural Engineering* [1]

CONTENTS

THE PRINCIPAL PURPOSE of this bulletin is to supply plans for low-cost farm dwellings designed to meet the requirements of the farm operator and his family. Some of the plans may be useful in cases where, in addition to the main dwelling, smaller homes are needed for relatives, tenants, or unmarried farm hands. Still others will be found useful in the construction of low-cost houses for temporary use.

A well-built farmhouse should last for 60 years or more. In the ordinary course of events at least two generations of children will be brought up in it. During these years the family operating the farm probably will have no other choice of dwelling. The builder should, therefore, think both of present needs and possible future requirements when selecting a plan for a new farmhouse.

FARMHOUSE REQUIREMENTS

SIZE

The first requirement of a satisfactory farmhouse is adequate size to provide needed working area, storage space, and living and sleeping quarters. For the average family at least three sleeping rooms are needed, [2] one for the parents, one for the boys, and one for the girls.

All the space may not be needed at the time the house is built, but the chances are that it will be needed before many years. On the other hand, many families find that after the children have

---

[1] Acknowledgment is made of the extended collaboration of Louise Stanley, Chief, Bureau of Home Economics, in selecting and reviewing the plans presented herein; and of the helpful assistance of W. H. Nash, architect, Bureau of Agricultural Engineering, in the preparation of both the manuscript and illustrations for publication. Mary Rokahr, senior home management specialist, Extension Service, and Eloise Davison, director of domestic electric service program, Electric Home and Farm Authority, made valuable suggestions regarding arrangement of kitchens and other equipment. Helpful comments and suggestions have been received from many other persons. Many of the perspective sketches illustrating the house plans shown in this bulletin were drawn by C. W. Mead, Bureau of Agricultural Engineering.

[2] Sometimes the living room must serve as one of the sleeping rooms.

grown up and left home it is not necessary to use the entire house. For this reason it is desirable to have it arranged so that part of the rooms may be closed off or may be rented to tourists.

COMFORT AND CONVENIENCE

Adequate, well-used space for both the family and the furniture is a large factor in farmhouse comfort. The proper number, size, and placement of windows, doors, and stairs, and good construction are important. These matters have been carefully worked out in the plans shown in this bulletin. Comfort also depends to a large extent on good heating, plumbing, lighting, and screening. Information on some of these subjects is given in Farmers' Bulletin 1698, Heating the Farm Home; 1448, Farmstead Water Supply; 1426, Farm Plumbing; 1227, Sewage and Sewerage of Farm Homes; Circular 406, Oil Burners for Home Heating; and in U. S. Department of Commerce bulletin, Insulation on the Farm, price 10 cents.

The convenient arrangement of the farmhouse begins with its relationship to the other farm buildings and to the highway. Unlike the city house, the farmhouse has its main line of communication through the back or side door. Therefore outside doors and porches should be located so as to give convenient entrance from the farm driveway and the path to the barn, and wherever possible should be on the sheltered side of the house.

If possible, there should be a convenient place near the rear entrance for men to leave their outer wraps and to wash before going into the house. These facilities are often provided in a washroom or in one corner of the workroom, but if there is no washroom or workroom in the house, there should at least be clothes hooks and a bench and washbasin for summer use on the back porch.

It is also desirable that the work portions of the house, where the housewife spends much of her time, look out over the farm buildings and the entrance roadway. Most farm women like also a glimpse of the highway from the kitchen window.

Preferably the traffic way from the rear entrance to the main portion of the house should not lead through the kitchen. If the kitchen must be used as a passageway, the doors should be so arranged that the traffic does not cross the work area. This not only decreases the possibility of interference with household activities but also makes possible a more compact and convenient arrangement of work equipment. An important factor is a workroom or porch, on about the same level as the kitchen, for laundry, canning, care of milk, and other farm activities and for supplementary food storage. This saves much clutter in the kitchen itself and contributes to more efficient arrangement.

At least one bedroom should be provided on the first floor of the farmhouse, not too far from the kitchen, so that small children or sick persons may be cared for conveniently. The bathroom should be convenient to both downstairs and upstairs bedrooms, but preferably on the first floor. A space for a bathroom is very desirable even if the fixtures cannot be put in at once.

Ample storage space should be provided for clothing, bedding and linen, wraps, food, dishes and utensils, cleaning equipment, toys, and fuel. In general, these needs have been met in the plans given in this bulletin by closets in halls and bedrooms, kitchen cabinets, shelves or pantries, and cellar storage. Closet, cabinet, and shelf space adds greatly to the convenience and comfort of a house and should not be omitted.[3]

In the smaller plans shown here, an alcove or an end of the kitchen is indicated for use as a dining area. In the larger plans, either a dining room or a space for dining in the living room is provided, and in most cases there is also space in the kitchen for "hurry-up" meals.

The following points have been kept in mind in planning the kitchens.

A sink in every house is recommended. Even when water must be carried into the house, the sink and drain add much to the convenience of the kitchen and may be installed very cheaply. Where running water is not available, a pump may be installed beside the sink. However, running water, hot and cold, adds more to the convenience of the farm home than almost any other factor.

The sink should be well lighted, with windows over or at one end of it. Windows over the sink should have the sills higher than the back of the sink. Such windows will need to be shielded from sun glare unless on the north side of the house. The sink should have a drain board at the left end, at the right a flat shelf for stacking dishes if there is no drain board there. Dish storage should be near enough the left end of the sink for the dishes to be put away without unnecessary steps.

The cookstove should be conveniently near the sink, preferably against the side wall, or across from it if the kitchen is narrow.

A small food-preparation surface, table or shelf, should be placed next to the stove at the same height as the cooking surface. There should be cupboard space near the stove for the storage of cooking utensils. A worktable should be provided for long mixing jobs; it should have knee space and toe space. Staple supplies should be stored near this table and, if possible, should be near the refrigerator and not too far from the stove.

The refrigerator should, for convenient use, be as near as possible to the worktable and stove; however, the higher the surrounding temperature the greater the cost of operating the refrigerator. If an ice refrigerator is used, a location near the outside door lessens the tracking of dirt into the house. A ventilated cupboard near the worktable is convenient for storing the less perishable foods and reduces the season during which ice is needed.

RELATION TO OTHER BUILDINGS AND HIGHWAY

A house designed for the south or west side of the highway should be reversed if it is to be built on the north or east. For example, plan 6521 (p. 24) would fit nicely on either the south or the west side of the main road. If it were south of the highway, with the drive as shown, the kitchen would be on the east where it would have the advantage of the morning sunlight and in most localities the

[3] Plans for closets and storage spaces can be obtained from the Bureau of Home Economics.

screened porch would be sheltered from the coldest winds. If the house were on the west side of the road, the kitchen would still get morning sunlight, and the porch would protect it from the afternoon sun. On the other hand, if the house were to be built on the north or east side of the road, the kitchen would be badly sheltered and lighted, but reversing the plan so that the kitchen would be on the right instead of the left side of the house would remedy these conditions.

Before deciding to build any house the plan should be studied carefully to see how it will best fit the location and the arrangement of the rest of the farmstead.

APPEARANCE

Attractive appearance of a farmhouse is to be obtained by:

Good taste in its proportions and exterior design.
Materials chosen to suit the local environment and type of house, effectively employed.
A pleasing color scheme for the house, in harmony with its surroundings.
Proper planning with relation to the natural features of the site, the other farm buildings, and the highway.
Grading the site and planting trees, shrubs, and flowers.

If the homes shown in this bulletin are carefully built according to the drawings, they will be satisfactory with respect to the first two points.

Proper location of the house is exceedingly important and must be worked out on the ground. Farmers' Bulletin 1132, Planning the Farmstead, and 1087, Beautifying the Farmstead, will be found helpful in this and in the planting of trees and shrubs around the house. Farmers' Bulletin 1452, Painting on the Farm, discusses kinds and uses of paints. Other bulletins on these subjects are available from several of the State agricultural colleges.

SAFETY

Safety in the farmhouse depends first on good construction for protection from damage by wind, fire, decay, and termites. Safety is promoted also by planning to avoid hazards from low beams, steep or unguarded stairways, or badly placed doors and windows. The working drawings for the houses illustrated herein embody good practice in these matters. The welfare and convenience of the occupants will be further permanently safeguarded through rat-proof construction, which eliminates " rat harbors ", and denies easy entrance of the rodents to the building. Additional safety may be secured at slight cost by following the recommendations in Farmers' Bulletins 1590, Fire Protective Construction on the Farm; 1638, Rat Proofing Buildings and Premises; and 1649, Construction of Chimneys and Fireplaces; Leaflet 87, Wind-Resistant Construction for Farm Buildings, and Leaflet 101, Injury to Buildings by Termites.

CONSTRUCTION MATERIALS

The houses shown in this bulletin may, with slight changes, be built of wood, stone, concrete, brick, tile, earth, steel, or other materials. The choice depends largely on owner's preference, local availability and price, and the skill of local builders in using one or another. Many new materials for various purposes such as roofing, flooring, and insulation are on the market and deserve consideration.

The practice common among farmers of hauling their own stone or concrete materials, cutting their own logs where possible, having their lumber sawed at local mills, and doing part of the actual construction work, aid in reducing the cash outlay and in making possible a better house for the same money expenditure. This is especially true where lumber is sawed long enough before building starts to allow thorough seasoning. This seasoning of lumber is important and is too often disregarded.

COSTS

The most satisfactory way to learn the probable cost of a house is to obtain estimates from one or more local builders. Approximate costs may, of course, be obtained by comparing the proposed house with one built recently in the same community, or rough estimates may be based on the size of the house and typical unit costs for the locality.

Unit costs based on prices and wages prevailing in the spring of 1934 for houses suitable for the localities were obtained for about 300 counties by the Farm Housing Survey. A summary of the figures is as follows:

CELLARS

Costs for ordinary cellars were reported for most sections as varying from 50 cents to $1 per square foot of floor space. The cost per square foot is, of course, less for a large than for a small cellar, other things being equal. Easy excavation and low-cost materials also make for low unit cost. Costs of nearly $2 per square foot were reported in some sections where the ground-water level is high and cellar walls and floor must be carefully waterproofed. In sections where cellars are not ordinarily used the cost of the foundation was reported as part of the cost of the house superstructure.

SUPERSTRUCTURES AND PORCHES

Reported costs of one-story frame superstructures, including heating, plumbing, and lighting equipment ordinarily used in the locality, ranged from $1.25 to $2.25 per square foot of floor space in the South, from $2.25 to $3.50 in the West and Southwest, from $2.50 to $4 in the North, and from $3 to $4.50 in New England. Costs in Maryland, Virginia, and West Virginia and in a narrow belt along the east coast, including Florida, were reported from $2 to $3.25, and in the timber-producing sections of the Northwest at about $2 per square foot. Costs in any locality are influenced by local factors, generally being relatively high near cities and in thickly settled sections and relatively low in places where there are local supplies of lumber or other materials.

Differences in cost between the various sections are due to differences in the kinds of houses built, as well as to differences in material costs and wages. The typical house in the North is much more compact and substantial and provided with more expensive heating equipment than the typical house in the South.

The cost per square foot of floor area of two-story frame houses was reported as being 5 to 15 percent less than that of one-story houses in the same locality.

The costs of typical masonry superstructures were generally reported at $2 to $3 per square foot of floor area in the southern third of the United States, from $3 to $4 per square foot in the central third, and more than $4 per square foot in the northern third of the country. There were many variations from these general levels, however, costs of about $2 per square foot being reported in many localities in the States bordering on or south of the Ohio River. Costs reported for counties along the Atlantic and Gulf coasts were generally higher than for those in the interior. Little difference in cost per square foot of floor area in one-story and in two-story masonry houses was reported. The higher costs reported for masonry houses as compared with frame are probably due in part to better grades of finish and equipment used in the masonry houses.

The costs per square foot of floor space of open porches were reported as being about half the costs per square foot of floor space in one-story houses of similar materials.

ESTIMATING BY UNIT COSTS

The floor areas of the cellar, the porches, and the house itself (the superstructure) are shown with each plan. They do not include unexcavated cellar space nor unfinished space in attics. The areas were figured from the working drawings (see p. 7) because in some cases the dimensions given in the plans herein are approximate only. The superstructure area of a house of more than one story is given here as the area of the first floor plus the usable area of the second floor. Stairways, halls, and closets are included. To estimate very roughly what a house might cost, multiply the number of square feet of cellar floor space by a cost per square foot based on the costs stated above. Do the same for the house superstructure and the porches, and add the figures together. This, with allowance for price changes since the spring of 1934, will give a rough estimate of total cost of the house. The actual cost will, of course, be affected by the materials and home equipment which the owner selects and by the skill and efficiency of the builders.

If the owner can furnish part of the material or labor, or if interior finish or equipment is omitted, the initial cash outlay may be reduced. Estimates based on local prices and wage rates are to be preferred to those based on the cost figures given above.

Little study has been given to what amounts farm people are justified in spending for their houses, but several investigations have been made of expenditures for housing by people with fixed incomes. It is generally agreed that the house ordinarily should not cost more than two and one-half times the average annual net income of the family. In the case of the farm family the value of the living furnished by the farm should be considered as part of the income. Another generally accepted rule, which perhaps is more nearly applicable to farm conditions, is that not more than 25 percent—usually not more than 20 percent—of the average annual net income of the family should be required for housing, including principal payments, interest, taxes, insurance, repairs, and miscellaneous costs.

WORKING DRAWINGS

Working drawings have been prepared giving all necessary dimensions and details for building these homes. Farmers may obtain copies of these drawings from the agricultural extension services of the State agricultural colleges. The State extension services will supply only those plans which are suitable in their respective States, and usually will make a small charge to cover printing and mailing.

CAUTION REGARDING CHANGES

These plans have been carefully prepared by competent architects in consultation with home-management specialists and agricultural engineers familiar with farm conditions in all parts of the United States. It is urged that the plans be studied carefully before making a selection, but that no changes be made in them except for alternate arrangements indicated by the drawings or descriptions. Changing the size of a room or the location of a door or window may spoil some other valuable feature, and is almost certain to harm the appearance of the house. Doors and windows should be selected according to the descriptive material on the drawings. Sizes should be closely adhered to for best appearance.

The prospective builder should not try to obtain too much originality, but rather should base his selection on those features of the plan which will give the utmost satisfaction in the long run. Differences in slope of ground, location of the drive and farm buildings, and position and amount of trees and shrubbery, all will contribute to the distinctive appearance of the home.

For homes of the type offered in this bulletin, the surroundings should be kept free from distracting adornments. As a general rule, a few trees to provide shade, some flowering shrubs of native growth grouped close to the building to break harsh lines, and a bed or two of flowers selected for their color value, will be sufficient decorative relief.

PLANS FOR HOUSES

The 40 house plans shown in this bulletin have been arranged in four groups representing, respectively, (1) 1-story growing houses; (2) 1-story houses originally built with two or more separate bedrooms; (3) houses of 1½ or 2 stories; and (4) very small houses. Some of the plans might have been placed in another group about as well as in that in which they are shown.

ONE-STORY GROWING HOUSES

There are many arguments in favor of the growing house for the farm. The first unit can be erected at a moderate cost, yet the finished house may have all the features considered important. As more space is needed the owner often can build the additions himself, taking advantage of slack times to cut lumber from his own land, haul sand and gravel for concrete, and in other ways reduce the cost of the additions. The chief difficulty with the growing house is that it is likely to grow very slowly. By the time additions are made the house is considered old by its occupants, and the additions are likely not to receive as careful attention as the original house.

The growing houses in this bulletin have been carefully planned so that both the first units and the final structure are satisfactory in usefulness and in appearance. The additions fit into the original units with a minimum of ripping out and rearrangement.

PLAN 6511,[4] FOR THE SOUTHWEST

Floor areas: Superstructure, first unit 605 square feet; with 1-bedroom addition 815 square feet; with 2-bedroom addition 960 square feet.

This plan is for a permanent dwelling of frame, stucco, stone,

adobe, or other construction. If desired, the first unit may be built without bedrooms, as shown, and the living room used for sleeping quarters until the house is completed. The two large closets of this living room add much to its

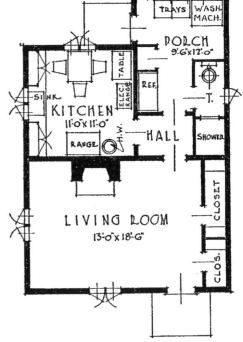

value, and the arrangement with all doors at one end of the room permits efficient use of the space.

If the first unit is to be used for several years before the bedrooms are added, the small bathroom with shower will be especially desirable. That space must be used for other purposes, however, and the bathroom fixtures moved when one or both bedrooms are added.

An alternate kitchen arrangement suggested by the Bureau of Home Economics for houses in which only an oil, gas, or electric stove is needed and meals will usually be eaten in the living-dining room is shown on page 9.

[4] Prepared by W. K. Bartges and Earl Barnett for the department of agricultural engineering, University of California.

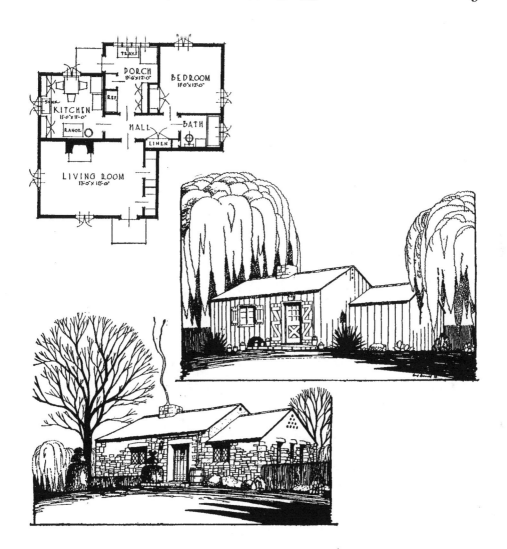

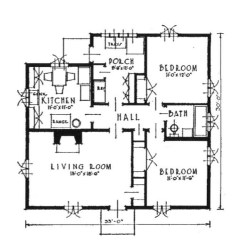

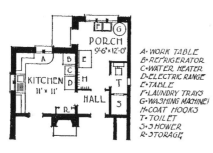

PORCH
9'-6" x 12'-0"

KITCHEN
11' x 11'

HALL

A· WORK TABLE
B· REFRIGERATOR
C· WATER HEATER
D· ELECTRIC RANGE
E· TABLE
F· LAUNDRY TRAYS
G· WASHING MACHINE
H· COAT HOOKS
T· TOILET
S· SHOWER
R· STORAGE

PORCH
9'-6" x 12'-0"

KITCHEN
11'-0" x 11'-0"

HALL

BEDROOM
11'-0" x 12'-0"

BATH

LIVING ROOM
13'-0" x 18'-6"

BEDROOM
11'-0" x 11'-0"

33'-0"

30'-0"

PLAN 6512,[5] FOR THE SOUTH

Floor areas: Superstructure, first stage 715 square feet; second stage with one bedroom 1,085 square feet; third stage 1,515 square feet. Porch, 250 square feet.

Plan 6512 is designed for southern conditions, to afford ample shade from a glaring summer sun. The arrangement of rooms permits the building to face toward the south, thus taking advantage

of the summer breezes from that direction. The glazed porch on the north side offers a cool spot for summer meals, while the meals served during cold weather would naturally be more enjoyable in front of a blazing fire at the west end of the living room.

The second stage of the house adds the center bedroom of the three shown in

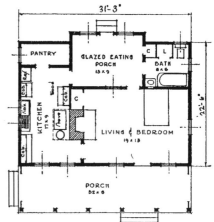

the third stage. The partitions for the hall and the closets near the south porch are not needed until the third stage. If at all possible, the center bedroom should be built with the original unit to provide more sleeping space; but if it is necessary to watch the budget closely, the large living room or the glazed porch can be pressed into temporary service as sleeping quarters.

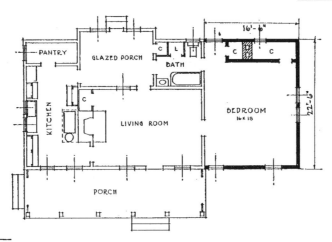

[5] Prepared by J. B. Atkinson and J. E. Hudson for the department of agricultural engineering, Agricultural and Mechanical College of Texas.

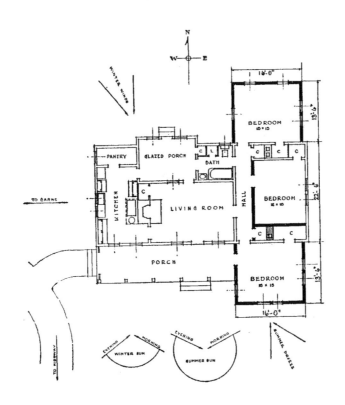

PLAN 6513,[6] FOR THE SOUTH

Floor areas: Superstructure, first unit 490 square feet; with first addition 705 square feet; completed house 1,015 square feet. Porches, first unit 25 square feet; with first addition 240 square feet.

The first unit of house 6513 is modest, and yet provides complete kitchen equipment, toilet facilities, a workroom or laundry, and a bedroom of comfortable size. The first addition increases the living accommodations and, with its front and rear porches, offers a cool retreat in hot weather. The second addition provides two more bedrooms and an adjoining bath, thus completing the six-room house. If desired, these two bedrooms may be made larger than shown in the plans.

The interior view shows the compact arrangement of kitchen cabinets and sink, and indicates the bright work area that is planned to lighten the duties of the housewife. An alternate arrangement of the kitchen, with no workroom, is shown on page 13.

During the first two stages of development adequate space will be found in the kitchen for dining; but when two bedrooms are added in the final wing, the original bedroom (adjoining the kitchen) might be converted into a dining room. On the other hand, if at times the entire house is not needed by the family, the last wing of the house will make very desirable rooms for renting to tourists or summer boarders, or may be closed.

In some parts of the South the fireplace will not provide sufficient heat in cold weather, but a circulator heater may be set in front of the fireplace and connected to the chimney through a metal shield. If the plan is used in the North, a cellar may be constructed under the second unit, with stairs leading down from the rear porch, which should be enclosed.

[6] Prepared by W. H. Nash for the Bureaus of Agricultural Engineering and Home Economics, U.S. Department of Agriculture.

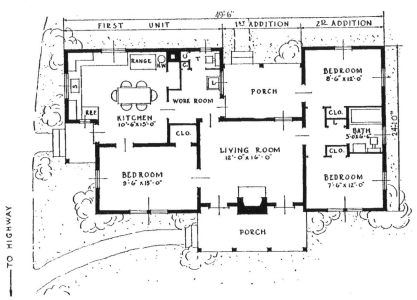

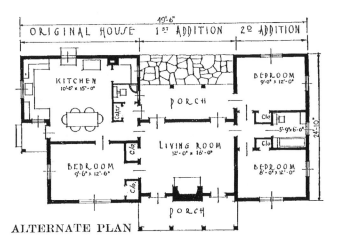

ALTERNATE PLAN

PLAN 6514,[7] FOR THE MIDDLE WEST

Floor areas: Superstructure, original house 670 square feet; with addition 940 square feet. Cellar, 255 square feet. Porches, 120 square feet.

House 6514, with basement and furnace, is well adapted to northern or mid-western conditions. The steps to the basement may be outside the building as shown, or the wash room may be extended so as to include the steps and provide greater protection during stormy weather.

The original house, in order to come in the class of low-cost houses, does not contain a bath. A pump at the kitchen sink provides water until funds permit of the installation of a modern plumbing system.

The first unit of the house may be heated either by a circulator heater in the living room or by a furnace. The furnace will be especially desirable after the second unit is added.

The added bedroom wing is recessed from the main building line to permit cross ventilation through the bedroom in the original house.

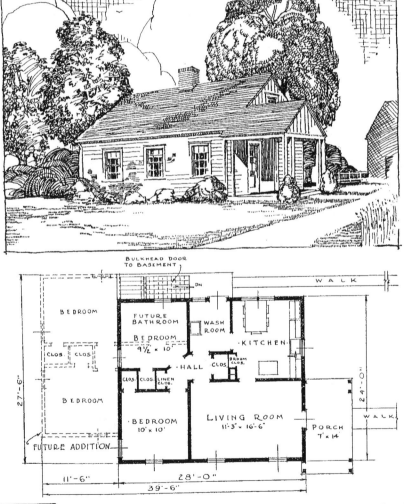

---

[7] Prepared by W. E. Pettit and Fred Riebel for the department of agricultural engineering, Ohio State University.

PLAN 6515,[8] FOR THE SOUTH

Floor areas: Superstructure, first unit 565 square feet; with first addition 900 square feet; completed house 1,255 square feet. Porches, 175 square feet.

This begins as a three-room house but is planned so that eventually three bedrooms and a bath may be added. The kitchen in the original house is nicely arranged, as shown in the plan. When the house is completed, the first bedroom may be used as a dining room, with a door cut through from the kitchen. The range should then be placed against the living-room wall. The fireplace and range will heat the first three rooms. Hall space for a circulator heater is provided in the first addition.

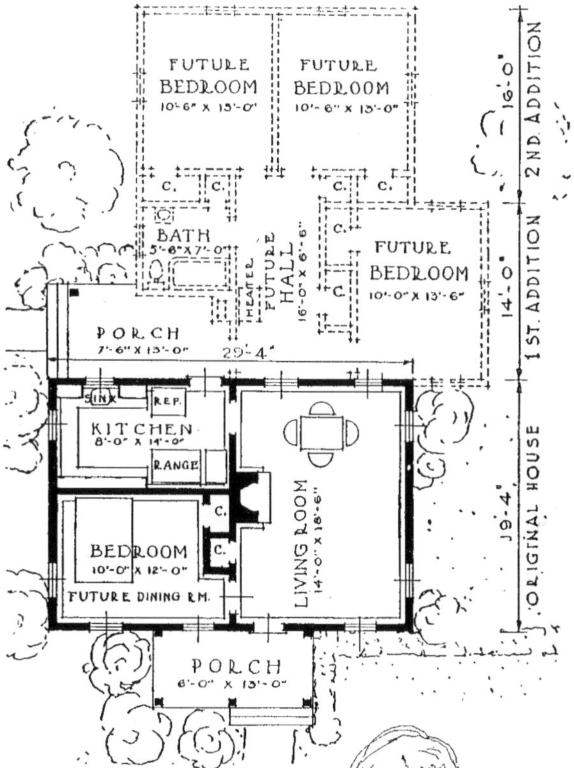

[8] Prepared by C. W. Heery, Fred J. Orr, and B. G. Danner for the department of agricultural engineering, University of Georgia.

100444°—35——3

PLAN 6516,[9] FOR THE SOUTH

Floor areas: Superstructure, original unit 685 square feet; with first addition 1,035 square feet; completed house 1,345 square feet. Porches, original 90 square feet; completed house 155 square feet.

The original unit of house 6516 is a two-room structure of ample size. The dining room and kitchen are combined in one room, while the other room is temporarily both bedroom and living room. A porch leading directly into the kitchen affords entrance during the initial stage. In the center of the first unit are an unusually large storage closet and a chimney reminiscent of colonial Virginia. In localities where firewood is not readily available the fireplace may be omitted and a stove used for heating the bedroom.

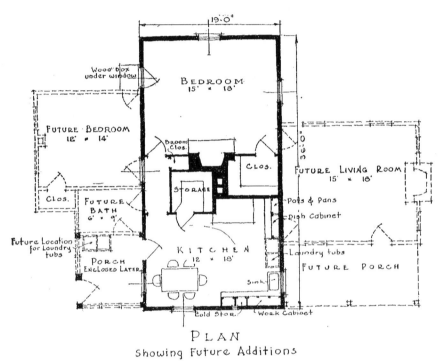

PLAN
Showing Future Additions

Additions to the house are indicated on both sides of the original; the first addition undoubtedly would be that with the bedroom and bath. The rear porch can be enclosed if needed, and will then serve for laundering and other work that is more convenient not to do in the kitchen. The second addition will complete the house with a living room and front porch.

The addition of the living room and front porch requires considerable change in the arrangement of the kitchen to keep traffic from the back door to the living room from passing directly in front of the range. It will be best to set the range against the end wall, and preferably to use an electric or oil range so that no new chimney will be required. After the living room is added, less dining space will be needed in the kitchen.

[9] Prepared by H. B. Boynton and J. M. Thompson for the department of agricultural engineering, Virginia Polytechnic Institute.

VIEW OF ORIGINAL UNIT

VIEW OF COMPLETED HOUSE

PLAN 6517,[10] FOR THE SOUTH

Floor areas: Superstructure, original house 660 square feet; completed house 1,025 square feet. Porches, 300 square feet.

In plan 6517 a large amount of space is provided at low cost by using the cheapest type of construction and omitting the interior finish at the time of building, for when a large family must be housed and funds are limited space is often more desirable than good finish and ease of heating. The exterior walls are of vertical boards and battens, and the roof is of galvanized corrugated metal. The house may be improved at any time by lining the walls and ceiling. The kitchen arrangement shows a treatment recommended by home economists, the sink and worktable at right angles to the wall, with shelves above them. This scheme has the advantage of separating the working and dining areas, yet it does not hamper easy communication between the rooms at meal hours. If desired, a bed may be placed in the living room, yet the house is so arranged that each sleeping room will have complete privacy. The side wall of the small bedroom next to the kitchen is intended to be made of 1-inch boards with battens on both sides.

The addition of bedrooms with closets and a bathroom is suggested. This addition will provide space for a circulator heater, which is a convenience when no cellar is planned.

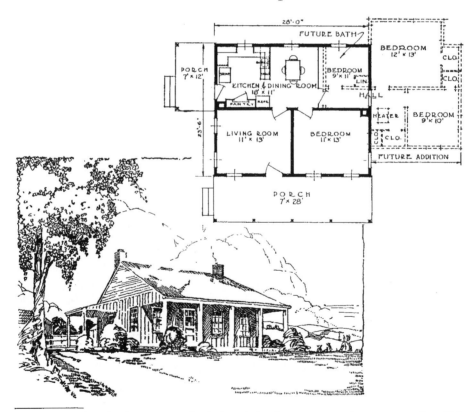

[10] Prepared by the Bureaus of Agricultural Engineering and Home Economics, U.S. Department of Agriculture.

PLAN 6518 [11]

Floor areas: Superstructure, first stage 835 square feet; with addition 1,160 square feet. Porches, 120 square feet.

Several novel features about this small dwelling will appeal to the farm-home builder. A heater room on the main floor near the rear entrance and the kitchen avoids the need for a cellar. A kitchen like this, with three outside walls to give light and cross ventilation and a better view of the farmstead and highway, is often desirable. The end of the living room next the kitchen is narrowed to a dining alcove, and when more space is needed the dining table may be extended into the living room. The completed bungalow has three bedrooms, with ample closet space. The rear porch will provide a comfortable, shady place to work outside during the warm summer days.

In the first stage of construction the two bedrooms at the rear may be omitted. This would still leave one bedroom and the bathroom and temporary closet space in the original bungalow. Then the two other bedrooms can be added later, when funds become available, or a screened and glazed sleeping porch with outside entrance could be built instead. A porch off the living room could also be added.

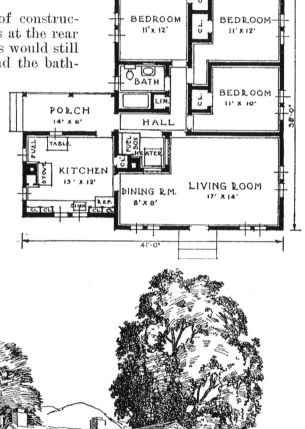

[11] Prepared by L. J. Smith for the department of agricultural engineering, State College of Washington.

PLAN 6519,[12] FOR THE SOUTHWEST

Floor areas: Superstructure, original house 775 square feet; with addition 1,075 square feet. Porches, 160 square feet.

The plans and perspectives on these pages show two methods of roofing this house. In each plan the original unit of the house is complete, and pleasing in appearance, and the additions fit the house gracefully with very little tearing out or rearrangement.

As in some other plans, the kitchen is designed for the use of an oil, gas, or electric cookstove. The house may be heated by a circulator hot-air heater, by a hot-water system with a radiator boiler in

[12] Prepared by H. E. Wichers, O. S. Ekdahl, and N. F. Resch for the department of architecture, Kansas State Agricultural College.

the living room, or possibly by radiant gas or electric heaters in the bedrooms.

The type of design favors keeping the house close to the ground. If floor-joist construction is used, the topsoil should be removed from under the house so that joists will not come too close to the ground surface. A concrete subfloor could be placed directly on the ground, supporting wood sleepers and wood floors.

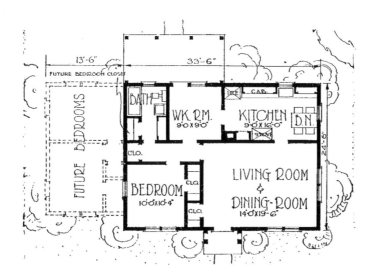

PLAN 6520[13]

Floor areas: Superstructure, first unit 450 square feet; with first addition 730 square feet; completed house 985 square feet. Porches, 255 square feet.

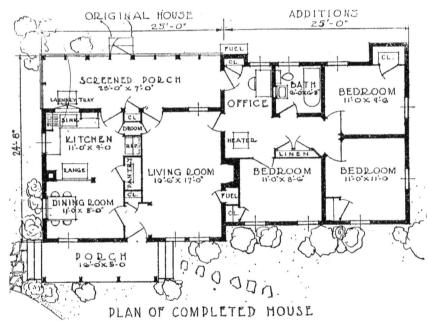

PLAN OF COMPLETED HOUSE

With their low-pitched roofs, and modest design both inside and out, plans 6520 and 6521 represent very desirable types of farmhouses. Such buildings blend with their surroundings to produce a real homey atmosphere. Originally planned for southern conditions, where a circulator heater placed in the hall should be adequate, these plans are adapted to colder regions if the houses are well constructed

[13] Prepared by Eldred Mowery and C. E. Cope for the Bureaus of Agricultural Engineering and Home Economics, U.S. Department of Agriculture.

PLAN 6521 [13]

Floor areas: Superstructure, first unit 630 square feet; with first addition 985 square feet; completed house 1,285 square feet. Porches, 385 square feet.

and are provided with basements and central heating plants as indicated on the working drawings.

In both designs the development from two large rooms progresses logically, the main difference being that in plan 6520 the additions are made at the side, while in plan 6521 the new rooms are added at the rear of the first unit. Although all the rooms of 6521 are shown as larger than those of 6520, by slight alterations either size of house may be built from either plan. The choice should be determined largely by the slope of the building site.

SCREENED PORCH
8'-0" x 15'-6"

COATS

STAIRS IF BASEMENT
IS DESIRED

LAUNDRY TRAYS

SINK

BR'MS.

FUEL

KITCHEN
14'-0" x 9'-6"

PANTRY

REF.

BEDROOM
7'-6" x 14'-0"

RANGE

OIL ST.

TEMPORARY

CL.

DINING ROOM
14'-0" x 9'-6"

BEDROOM
12'-6" x 14'-0"

CL.

PORCH
8'-0" x 31'-6"

FLOOR PLAN OF FIRST UNIT

[13] Prepared by Eldred Mowery and C. E. Cope for the Bureaus of Agricultural Engineering and Home Economics, U.S. Department of Agriculture.

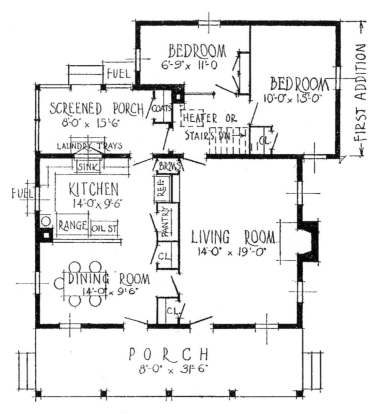

In each original house a temporary partition provides 2 bedrooms in place of a living room. The first addition adds 2 other bedrooms, and the removal of the partition between the temporary bedrooms provides a large living room. The second addition increases the total number of bedrooms to 3 by adding 2 and refitting 1 in the first addition as a bathroom.

Each kitchen is ideally located to command a view of the driveway, highway, and farm buildings. Closets, pantry, and other equipment utilize the darker part of the room, leaving the lighter portions for working area and dining table. These arrangements are complete in the original house.

On the screened back porch, which is equipped with laundry trays and closet, men coming from the fields may hang their outside work garments and, except in cold weather, wash before entering the house. Here a great deal of the dirty and messy work in preparing fruits and vegetables for canning may be done. Entrance from the screened porch to the bath or bedrooms reduces to a minimum the traffic through the kitchen and living room. In plan 6520 the screened porch might be divided by a lattice into work and living spaces.

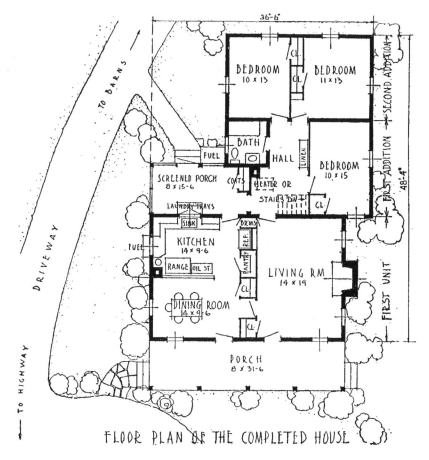

FLOOR PLAN OF THE COMPLETED HOUSE

PLAN 6522 [11]

Floor areas: Superstructure, original house 640 square feet; with addition *A* 950 square feet; with addition *B* 930 square feet. Porch, addition *B*, 120 square feet.

On account of its compact arrangement, this low-cost house furnishes a very satisfactory amount of usable space for the small family and may be enlarged to three-bedroom size, as indicated on the plans. The kitchen is well arranged, with moderate storage space, and a wood box filled from outside, with a ventilated cupboard or cooler above it. The workroom, unusually large for a small house, is a good place for laundry or canning and for men to clean up before coming in to meals. Dining space is provided at the rear of the living room. This house should be compared with no. 6527 (p. 36).

Board and batten construction is very suitable for a low-cost house, but any other type of construction may be used for plan 6522 if preferred. If the house is built in a cold climate, probably it will be desirable to omit the fireplace and heat the living and bedrooms with a circulator heater.

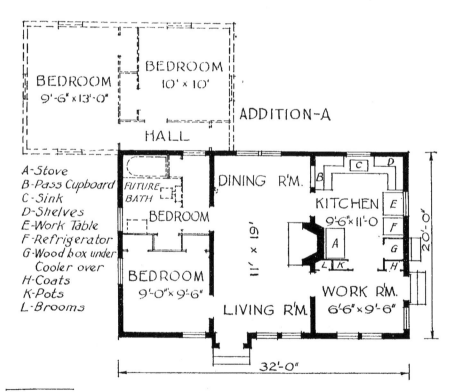

A-Stove
B-Pass Cupboard
C-Sink
D-Shelves
E-Work Table
F-Refrigerator
G-Wood box under
   Cooler over
H-Coats
K-Pots
L-Brooms

[14] Prepared by the Bureaus of Agricultural Engineering and Home Economics, U.S. Department of Agriculture.

PLAN 6523,[15] FOR THE SOUTH

Floor areas: Superstructure, first unit 990 square feet; with addition *A* 1,420 square feet; with addition *B* 1,375 square feet. Cellar, 350 square feet. Porches, 100 square feet.

Communication between rooms is an important consideration in modern house planning. This has been provided in house 6523 by a small hall, which permits access not only from one room to another but also to the outside, the basement stairs, the wash room, the bathroom, and the linen closet, thus eliminating the necessity of using any room as a passageway.

Alternate extensions are shown, the choice probably depending upon the surrounding ground contour. Addition *B* should receive first consideration, because it brings the two new bedrooms into closer relation with the bathroom and does not destroy the wash room adjoining the rear entrance. It does, however, reduce the size of one of the first bedrooms.

If addition *A* is contemplated, the window at *X* should be located at *Y* when the first unit is built. The steps in the hall of addition *A* may be omitted if the ground slopes down at the rear so that the floor of the addition can be built at a lower level than the floor of the original house.

If addition *B* is to be used, the window at Z should be located so as to come in the hall of the addition.

---

[15] Prepared by C. W. Heery and B. G. Danner for the department of agricultural engineering, University of Georgia.

The original house is compact and of pleasing design. The high sloping roof with louvers in the gables affords air circulation to aid in keeping the house cool in warm climates. The attic space may be used for storage; it is reached by stairs over those to the cellar or through a trap door in the ceiling. There is also space for a good-sized room in the attic over the bathroom, but if such a room is wanted the ceiling joists should be made 2 by 8 inches, instead of 2 by 6 inches as specified in the working drawings, the walls and ceiling of the room should be insulated for comfort both in summer and in winter, and a double window in the end wall and a dormer window at the rear should be provided, to give cross ventilation.

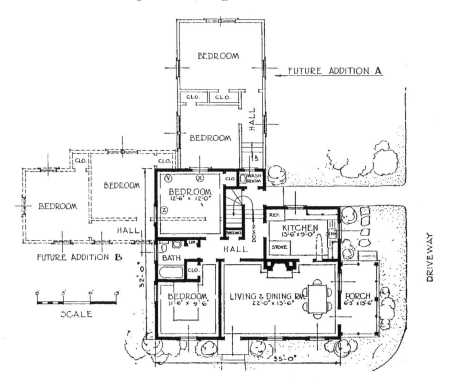

The working drawings provide for a piped warm-air furnace in the cellar, which occupies one corner of the space under the house. If no cellar is wanted, the stairs could be omitted and the original house, without the additions, could be heated nicely by a circulator heater in the hall. In this case the fireplace should be moved about 18 inches to the left to give a flue connection in the hall.

PLAN 6524[16]

Floor areas: Superstructure, first unit 1,245 square feet; with addition 1,735 square feet. Porches, 25 square feet. Cellar, 400 square feet.

The charm of house 6524 lies in its informality and simplicity. It is built for comfort and service. The broad expanse of roof, relieved by a gable, gives it a substantial yet homelike appearance. This is an easy house to move around in, and the kitchen is very nicely arranged. The screened porch, in addition to providing a cool and inviting summer dining and work space, affords ready access to all the rooms of the house. If the future addition of bed-

rooms is contemplated, the hall window in the first unit should be replaced with a door. This will not only provide an extra exit from the house but obviate unnecessary cutting and tearing out when the addition is built.

The cellar provides space for a central heating plant, if desired.

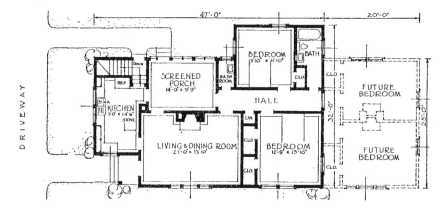

[16] Prepared by C. W. Heery, Fred J. Orr, and B. G. Danner for the department of agricultural engineering, University of Georgia.

The interior view shows the efficient kitchen arrangement and ample cabinet space planned for this house. Note that the sink drainboard is at the left for most convenient work by the average right-handed person, and that there is ample space for stacking soiled dishes at the right of the sink. The broad work shelf is 35 inches above the floor—a good average height—and there is toe space at the front for comfort while standing. The space under the sink is left clear so that the housewife may sit comfortably on a stool for the longer jobs.

All the cabinets are shown with doors, which aid in keeping out dust and add to the neat appearance of the kitchen. However, the main purpose of the cabinets is to provide ample work surface and shelf space, and if money is scarce the first economy should be to omit the upper doors. They may be added later, or a roller window shade may be mounted above the shelves and drawn down to cover them when not in use.

PLAN 6525 [17]

Floor areas: Superstructure, first unit 795 square feet; with bedroom addition 1,080 square feet; with both additions 1,375 square feet. Porches, 105 square feet. Cellar, 795 square feet.

This simple farmhouse develops into a home of dignity and charm. The original unit furnishes all modern conveniences and an ample basement. Future bedrooms may be added as required, while the extended living room might be built as the final touch of growing prosperity.

It will be of interest to the reader to note the similarity of arrangement of this house and no. 6519 (p. 20). These plans were developed independently, but the coincidence emphasizes the practicability of having the work and living areas on the side of the building next to the driveway and the bedrooms toward the rear, with the bathroom located as centrally as possible. The design of a small house for farm use is greatly influenced by the rather fixed location of the kitchen.

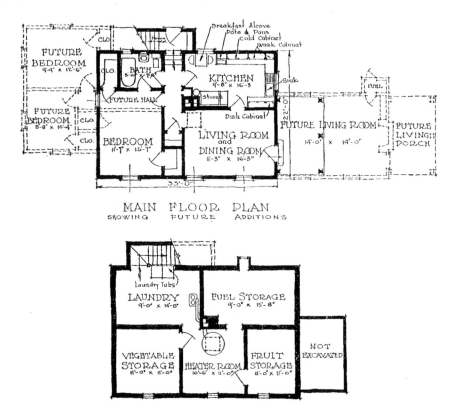

MAIN FLOOR PLAN
SHOWING   FUTURE   ADDITIONS

BASEMENT PLAN

[17] Prepared by H. B. Boynton and J. M. Thompson for the department of agricultural engineering, Virginia Polytechnic Institute.

VIEW OF ORIGINAL UNIT

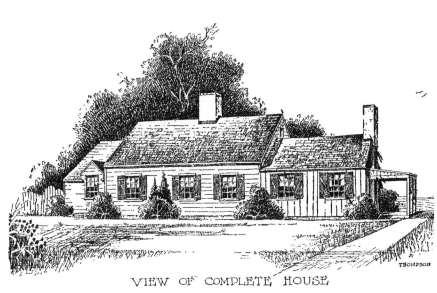

VIEW OF COMPLETE HOUSE

MODERATE-SIZED ONE-STORY HOUSES

Houses of this group can best be built complete at one time, though in several cases it is noted that rooms may be omitted from the original building or extra rooms added. The larger houses of this group provide about the same features as the completed growing houses. The more compact two-bedroom houses are well adapted to farms where two or more separate dwellings are needed.

PLAN 6526,[18] FOR TIMBERED SECTIONS

Floor areas; Superstructure, 845 square feet. Porches, 300 square feet.

In spite of present-day improvements in building materials, there is something about the rugged appearance of a log cabin that harmonizes with rural settings. Log construction blends into wooded surroundings more intimately than boards, bricks, or stucco.

House 6526 will accommodate 4 persons comfortably, or even 5 or 6 persons if a couch is placed in a corner of the living room.

The location of the bathroom not only serves the bedrooms but is convenient to the kitchen and the rear porch.

The central chimney serves the kitchen range, circulator heater, and fireplace. The ample size of the kitchen, and its built-in cup-

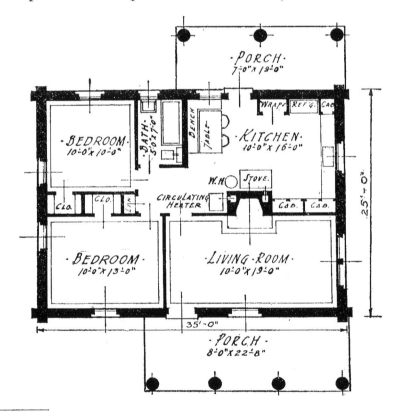

[18] Prepared by N. G. Napier for the department of agricultural engineering, University of Arkansas.

boards, dish cabinets, and other conveniences add greatly to the desirability of the design. If a pass cupboard between kitchen and living room is desired, it may be arranged in the cabinet next to the outer wall.

Many of the houses shown in this bulletin could be built of logs, with little change in detail. Farmers' Bulletin 1660, The Use of Logs and Poles in Farm Construction, describes several methods of using logs. The illustrations below show the economical use of slabs and flattened logs. The edges of the slabs should be cut to make close joints (a) and sill thickness should equal that of floor and quarter round (b). With horizontal flattened logs, at corners the projecting log should be notched to obtain a tight joint (c), and the projection sloped to shed water (d). This method of using slabs for walls was suggested by the University of Wisconsin.

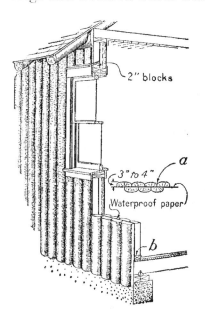

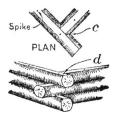

PLAN 6527 [19]

Floor areas: Superstructure, main house, 915 square feet; with storage addition 1,120 square feet. Cellar, 115 square feet. Porches, 130 square feet.

This house is similar in many respects to the first unit of 6522 (p. 26), but is enlarged to provide for the bathroom. A shallow root cellar with room above is added at the rear of the house to provide extra storage if needed in localities where a cellar is not practicable. As in the case of plan 6522, two more bedrooms may be added to the left side of the house by taking space from the rear bedroom for a hallway.

The house is planned to be heated by a jacketed heater in the workroom with a cold-air return duct under the floor and cold-air registers in the living room and bedrooms. This arrangement will keep all handling of coal and ashes out of the living parts of the house.

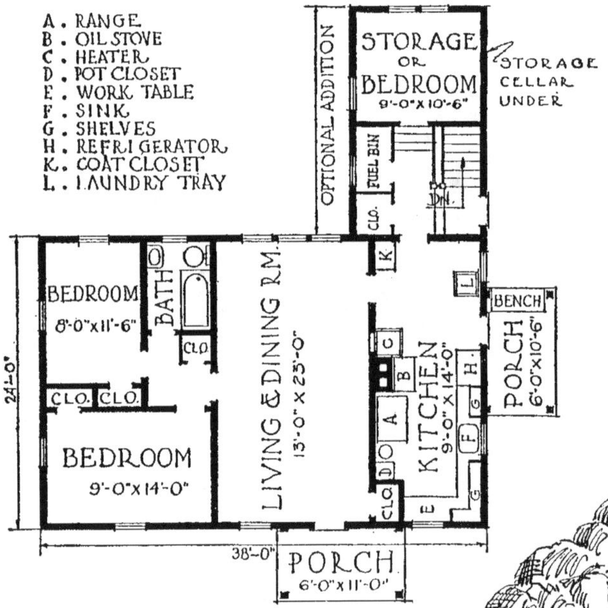

A . RANGE
B . OIL STOVE
C . HEATER
D . POT CLOSET
E . WORK TABLE
F . SINK
G . SHELVES
H . REFRIGERATOR
K . COAT CLOSET
L . LAUNDRY TRAY

PLAN 6528,[20] FOR THE NORTH

Floor areas: Superstructure, 800 square feet. Cellar, 800 square feet.

House 6528 is intended for use in cold, snowy regions, where farmers need cellars for storing fuel and vegetables. The hip roof helps to brace the house against the wind and is economical of material. A well-insulated ceiling is recommended to help keep the house comfortable. The substantial chimney in the center of the house, with separate flues for furnace, kitchen range, and fireplace, insures good draft and no wasted heat. The vestibule at the front and the hall arrangement at the side door also aid in keeping the house warm. Both doors are convenient to the driveway and the path to the barn.

The wash room and laundry of this house are in the cellar. This is a satisfactory and economical arrangement where there is good drainage for both the cellar and the plumbing fixtures, and is particularly advantageous on rolling ground. But one should beware of putting a deep cellar in a poorly drained location. (See Farmers' Bulletin 1572, Making Cellars Dry.)

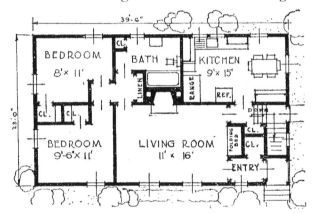

PLAN 6529 [21]

Floor areas: Superstructure, 740 square feet. Porches, 250 square feet.

This house was designed to meet the needs of a family of 4 to 6 people. The porch faces the highway, and paths from the front and side porches lead to the farm drive.

The kitchen is complete and compact. The extra space found in many farm kitchens has been omitted and a workroom added to provide for laundry and other rough work. This also provides a place for men to leave their outer wraps and wash before entering the living room. Storage space can be obtained in the attic by the use of a disappearing stair in the workroom ceiling.

No wood or coal range is provided for in this plan, because the use of an oil, gas, or electric stove saves space in the kitchen and correspondingly reduces the cost of the house. This saving and the convenience of a small, compact cooking unit deserve careful consideration in localities where these fuels are cheaply available. Heating is accomplished by means of a circulator heater in the living room.

The designer of this plan states:

The bedrooms are small. They are little used during waking hours, thus they can be reduced with less injury to family comfort than any other room. The large living room more than compensates for this.

When funds are limited it is always debatable, in a great portion of the United States, whether spending money for a porch is wise, because the same money could be used instead to increase the area of the house proper. In this particular case the porch could be left off without harm.

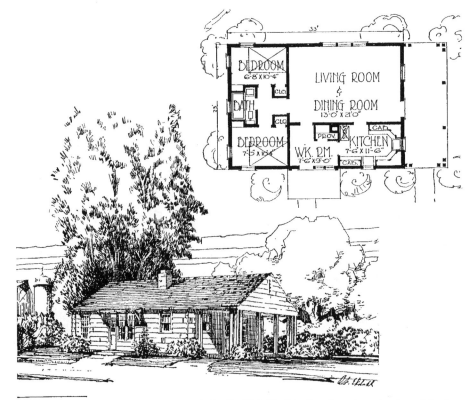

---

[21] Prepared by H. E. Wichers and O. S. Ekdahl for the department of architecture, Kansas State Agricultural College.

PLAN 6530 [22]

Floor areas: Superstructure, 1,155 square feet. Porches, 245 square feet.

The well-known economy of square house construction is illustrated by this plan. A choice of heating methods without a cellar is indicated. If a circulator heater is used in the hall, as shown, the chimney between the bedrooms will not be needed, and if extra bedrooms are wanted they may be added as in plan 6517 (p. 18). A fireplace in the back bedroom would, of course, interfere with taking a hall off this room.

Kitchen doors are located to permit easy communication between the screened porch and the hall without interference with the work area while the screened porch is useful as both work and dining area.

This latter feature, together with the ample size of the bedrooms, living room, and kitchen, makes the dwelling especially suitable for the small family in the South. The addition of a cellar under one-half of the house and of a central heating plant would adapt this plan to other sections of the country, though the rooms are rather larger than is common in the North.

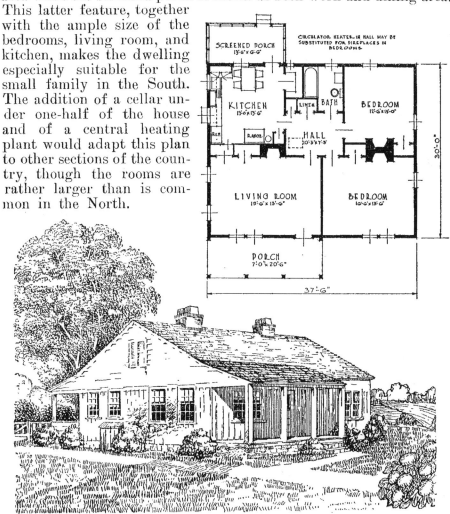

---

[22] Prepared by W. C. Breithaupt and H. W. Dearing for the department of agricultural engineering, Alabama Polytechnic Institute.

PLAN 6531 [23]

Floor areas: Superstructure, 1,185 square feet. Porches, 155 square feet.

House 6531 should be compared with no. 6533. The two plans were developed independently, but are very similar and illustrate a logical grouping of rooms for a farmhouse. In some respects the arrangement of 6531 works out more satisfactorily because it is not restricted by the structural details of framing a pitched roof.

This house is a model of compactness and efficiency. Note the simple but effective way in which the kitchen and heater room are located back to back. The floor of the heater room is a concrete slab, two steps below the main floor level. A pass cupboard between the kitchen and dining room is handy for serving meals. It also provides storage space beneath its counter. The entire bedroom side may be omitted from the original house, in which case the workroom would serve for dining and the dining room for a bedroom.

All dimensions of this house are multiples of 3½ feet. Wall, door, and window sections might be prefabricated so that erection would consist merely of bolting the sections together, or the house can be built in the ordinary way. The sketch at the top of page 41 illustrates the use of sheet metal as an exterior covering, the one in the center shows concrete blocks, and the bottom view shows the walls covered with a combination of lap siding and shingles or wide boards.

The flat roof should be covered with good roofing and well insulated for comfort in both summer and winter as described in the working drawings. The cost of the insulated flat roof should not be greater than that of an ordinary pitched roof without insulation. The accumulation of snow will help to keep the building warm.

---

[23] Prepared by Albert Frey for the Bureaus of Agricultural Engineering and Home Economics, U.S. Department of Agriculture.

PLAN 6532[24]

Floor areas: Superstructure, 1,125 square feet. Porches, 35 square feet.

This is a new type of low-cost house designed to provide five small single bedrooms or sleeping compartments and one bedroom of average size. The sleeping compartments are not very large, but to secure privacy and yet maintain economy of construction, something must be sacrificed. In this case it is unnecessary space.

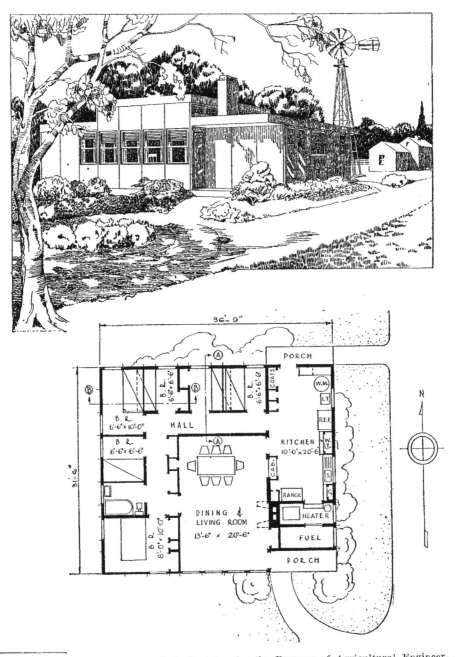

[24] Prepared by Albert Frey and R. G. Allen for the Bureaus of Agricultural Engineering and Home Economics, U.S. Department of Agriculture.

The sketch showing the arrangement of bunks illustrates an interesting feature of this house. In the right-hand room the bunk is near the floor, and wardrobe and dresser space is obtained in the partition between the two rooms. In the left-hand room the bunk is 4 feet above the floor and projects over the one on the other side of

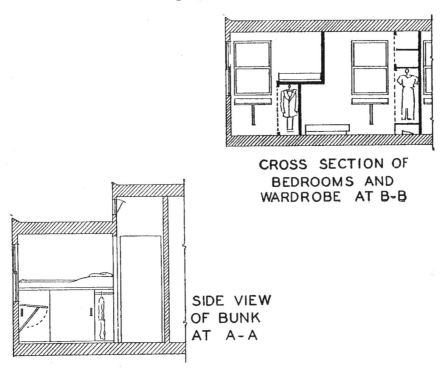

CROSS SECTION OF
BEDROOMS AND
WARDROBE AT B-B

SIDE VIEW
OF BUNK
AT A-A

the partition. Wardrobe space is arranged under the bunk. This room is especially suitable for a boy. A folding study table is provided under the window in each room. On warm nights air circulation would be obtained by opening the bedroom doors to the hall, which is ventilated by the windows above the lower roof. By omitting all but one of the partitions forming the five small bedrooms two good-sized rooms can be obtained.

The exterior appearance may seem, at first glance, unusually severe, but by omitting a pitched roof and the ornamental features of cornice moldings and trim decorations, the cost of construction is materially lowered. Here everything has been reduced to the simplest form possible.

With the heater room adjoining the kitchen, there is little need for a basement, thus an important item of expense is eliminated. The kitchen and workroom form a compact and very convenient unit along the driveway side of the house, while the large living room commands a good view of the highway. The living room and halls are lighted and ventilated by the small windows above the lower roofs. Closet space is provided in every room.

As in plan 6531 (p. 40), all dimensions are multiples of 3½ feet so that the house can be either prefabricated or built in the ordinary way.

PLAN 6533 [25]

Floor areas: Superstructure, 1,130 square feet. Porch, 80 square feet. Cellar, 280 square feet.

House 6533 is one of the few designs in which a separate dining space was allotted. Many people do not consider a separate dining room essential in the small farmhouse, and additional space adds to the cost, but in this case the arrangement adds to the spaciousness of the interior without greatly increasing the cost.

The rear entry is large enough to serve as laundry and washroom, and constitutes a back way from the kitchen to the bedrooms and bathroom without passing through the living room.

The kitchen, with cross ventilation and ample cupboard and counter space, is a pleasant workshop for the housewife, and is so arranged that easy service to the dining alcove is possible.

The bedrooms and adjoining bath are grouped together, allowing that portion of the house to be closed off from the living portion.

In the cellar is the heating plant, with fuel bin.

The house is kept low to give it an appearance of hugging the ground, but in no case should the joists be below the ground level. Shingles, beveled siding, or clapboards may be used for the exterior surface.

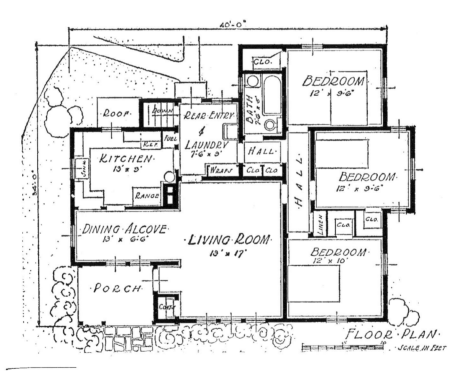

FLOOR PLAN.
SCALE IN FEET

---

[25] Prepared by Max Uhlig for the department of agricultural engineering, Massachusetts Agricultural College.

HOUSES OF MORE THAN ONE STORY

In many respects houses of more than one story are better suited for farm use in the Northern States than single-story buildings. They are more economical in foundation and roof construction, and are easier to heat. They should be arranged with one bedroom and a bath, or at least a toilet, on the ground floor. A cellar for fuel and vegetable storage and a central heating plant are usually needed with this type of house. The laundry may also be located in the cellar if suitable drainage and a grade door to the outside can be obtained, but in a poorly drained location it is best to keep the laundry above-ground. In building a cellar advantage should be taken of the slope of the ground to obtain good lighting and an easy entrance on the low side of the slope.

To avoid uncomfortably warm second-floor bedrooms in summer cross ventilation should be provided in each room. Insulation of the ceiling is valuable both in summer and in winter.

It is very convenient to have a bathroom on the second floor as well as one on the first floor, especially if rooms are to be rented to tourists when the family does not need the whole house.

PLAN 6534[26]

Floor areas: Superstructure, original house, 1,420 square feet; with living-room addition, 1,720 square feet. Cellar, 775 square feet. Porches, 285 square feet.

The first-floor and cellar plans of house 6534 are almost the same as the original unit of no. 6525 (p. 32), but there are comfortable

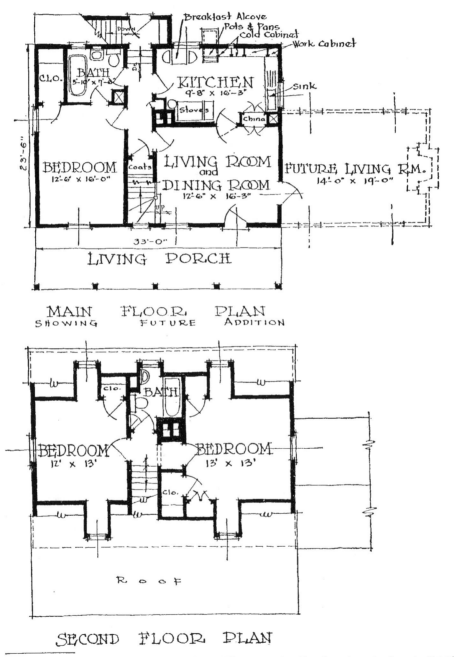

MAIN FLOOR PLAN
SHOWING FUTURE ADDITION

SECOND FLOOR PLAN

[26] Prepared by H. B. Boynton and J. M. Thompson for the department of agricultural engineering, Virginia Polytechnic Institute.

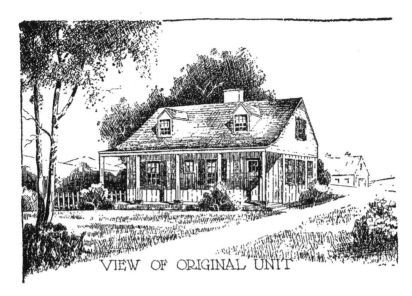

VIEW OF ORIGINAL UNIT

bedrooms, a bath, and closet space on the second floor. If funds are available to build the living-room wing indicated, the entire dwelling will breathe the traditional southern spirit of hospitable spaciousness.

The hall and stair arrangements of this house are very good. Persons coming in at the back door can leave wraps in the vestibule at the head of the cellar stairs and go directly to any downstairs room or to the cellar, yet there is little lost space.

If the house should at some time be occupied by a small family, the entire upstairs could be shut off. Persons wishing rooms for tourists will find either the upstairs bedrooms or the downstairs bedroom and bath very suitable for this purpose.

VIEW OF COMPLETE HOUSE

PLAN 6535 [27]

Floor areas: Superstructure, 820 square feet. Porch, 30 square feet.

This might well be considered the smallest story-and-a-half farmhouse that could be practicably built. The designer has utilized the space to good advantage, omitting a bath in the original structure for the sake of economy. The working drawings show a future addition to the house which provides a bedroom and bath on the first floor. The alternate floor plan shows a dormer in the rear like the one on the front, to make room for a second-floor bath.

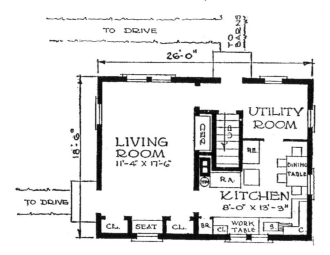

· FIRST · FLOOR · PLAN ·

A distinctive feature of this compact design is the L-shaped kitchen with its well-grouped and well-lighted working surfaces and dining table. The arrangement of an L-shaped room is often a problem when enlarging or remodeling. The living room is arranged for both day and night use, with a folding bed in a closet.

[27] Prepared by C. T. Bridgman for the department of agricultural engineering, Iowa State College.

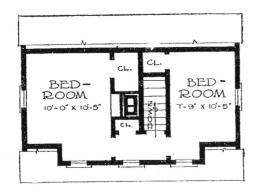

SECOND · FLOOR · PLAN ·

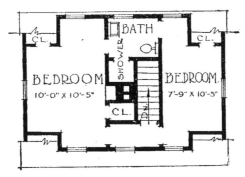

ALTERNATE
·SECOND · FLOOR · PLAN ·

ALTERNATE
·FIRST· FLOOR ·PLAN·

PLAN 6536,[28] FOR THE NORTH

Floor areas: Superstructure, 1560 square feet. Cellar, 400 square feet. Porch, 210 square feet.

This design illustrates a type of farmhouse frequently built in recent years because of its simple lines and economy of construction. It illustrates the pleasing possibility of fitting the farmhouse to sloping ground, with ample light in the basement and easy flights of steps between the house proper, the large workroom at the rear, and the cellar.

The partition between the main rooms downstairs is carried up to divide the second floor, giving these bedrooms ample size and good cross ventilation and making a strong construction that will not sag in years to come. A second bathroom may be provided in the storage space by the chimney, thus adding to the comfort of the home and making the upstairs rooms suitable for rental to tourists if desired. The roof should be insulated to give comfort both in summer and in winter.

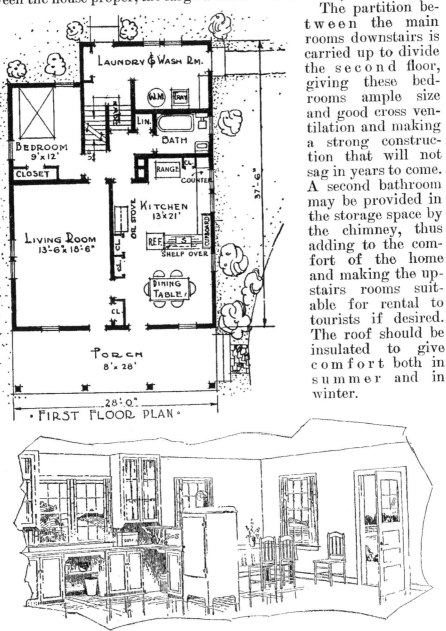

[28] Prepared by C. J. Poiesz and Eldred Mowery for the Bureaus of Agricultural Engineering and Home Economics, U.S. Department of Agriculture.

The downstairs hall, lighted by the windows on the stairs, is compact and provides easy communication between all rooms. The living room is well lighted and has good wall spaces for furniture. The combined kitchen and dining room, with the sink at right angles to the outside wall, as shown in the interior view, gives the housewife three walls of continuous work surfaces and in addition light and the view from all the windows of the room. Children can play or older members visit in the dining end with slight interference to the housewife's work. This is especially helpful on chilly days in the fall and spring when the kitchen stove provides the only heat in the house.

The part basement furnishes space for a furnace and for storage of fruits and vegetables.

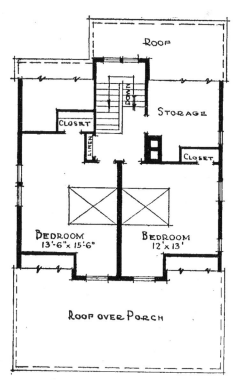

• SECOND FLOOR PLAN •

PLAN 6537[29]

Floor areas: Superstructure (including enclosed porch) 1,520 square feet. Cellar, 840 square feet. Terrace and steps, 100 square feet.

House 6537 is similar in many respects to no. 6536, and has much the same advantages, though the rooms are somewhat smaller. A second downstairs bedroom can be added beside the bathroom, if needed, or the two bedrooms on the second floor can be left unfinished if funds are not on hand to complete the building in the beginning.

The sketch indicates the roof line sweeping down snug over the window of the first-floor bedroom, a feature which is carried out with similar success in plan 6538. Designs of this type help to keep a two-story home from appearing too tall and make it a more harmonious unit in the farmstead scheme.

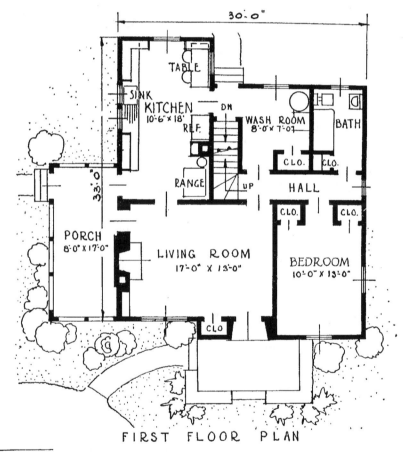

FIRST FLOOR PLAN

[29] Prepared by T. A. Zink for the department of agricultural engineering, Purdue University.

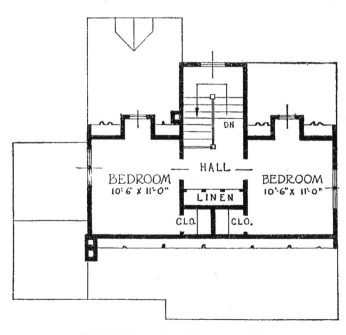

SECOND FLOOR PLAN

PLAN 6538 [30]

Floor areas: Superstructure, 1,740 square feet.   Cellar, 385 square feet. Stoops, 80 square feet.

House 6538 may be roofed in a number of ways, with slight alterations in the arrangement of the second floor.   The appearance is, of course, greatly altered; but in each case is pleasing.   With the modernistic flat roof, any waste spaces caused by the sloping roofs in the other designs are eliminated.   The storage room on the second floor then becomes suitable for a child's bedroom, a sewing room, or an

office, and the flat-deck porch roof will serve as a sleeping porch.

The plan is simple and well proportioned.   Since the arrangement of the entrance is a little unusual, the location of the driveway and the path to the barn should be given careful study before deciding upon the site and placing of the house.

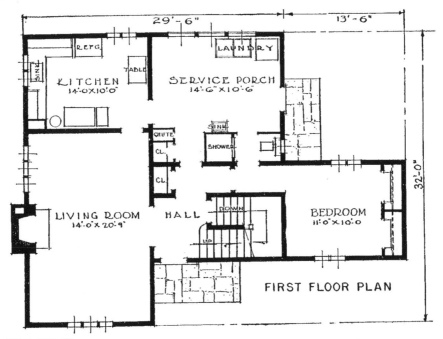

FIRST FLOOR PLAN

---

[30] Prepared by W. K. Bartges and Earl Barnett for the department of agricultural engineering, University of California.

Construction should be simple. In the case of the modernistic house, concrete or stucco is suggested for the first story and boards and battens for the second.

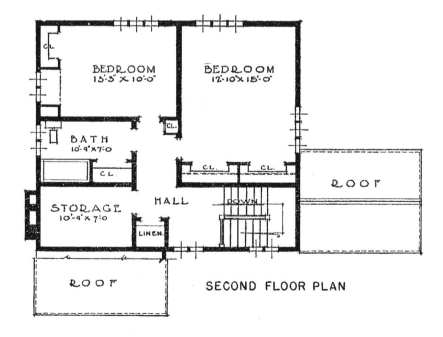

SECOND FLOOR PLAN

PLAN 6539,[31] FOR THE NORTH

VIEW OF FIRST STAGE

Floor areas: Superstructure, original house, 1,100 square feet; with kitchen addition, 1,270 square feet; with all additions shown, 1,620 square feet. Porches, original house, 90 square feet; completed house, 285 square feet. Cellar, 565 square feet.

Thousands of farmhouses in all parts of the North and Middle West have begun like house 6539, and the development illustrated for this one should offer helpful suggestions both to farmers who plan to build new and those who expect to remodel present houses. It is a very practical design, expressing honest dignity.

The plans on this page show the original

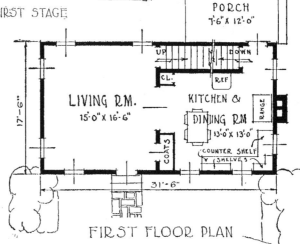

FIRST FLOOR PLAN

SECOND FLOOR PLAN

unit, which would supply a comfortable yet economical dwelling, with a basement for fuel and storage. The first addition might be either the new kitchen and porch or the downstairs bedroom, bath, and laundry. If needed, a third upstairs bedroom and a bathroom can be added over those in the first-floor addition, as shown in the working drawings, with little loss of material or work, because the downstairs bedroom has a flat-deck roof. This would increase the floor area of the superstructure to 1,900 square feet.

[31] Prepared by J. M. Deibert for the Bureaus of Agricultural Engineering and Home Economics, U.S. Department of Agriculture.

VIEW OF COMPLETED HOUSE

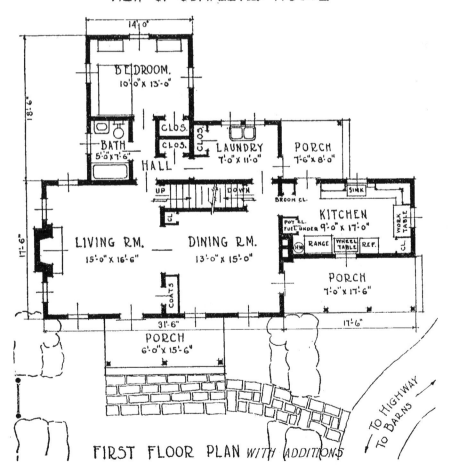

FIRST FLOOR PLAN *WITH ADDITIONS*

PLAN 6540 [32]

Floor areas: Superstructure, 1,380 square feet. Porch, 70 square feet. Cellar, 760 square feet.

This plan is intended for use in the North, where the compact floor plan with cellar and inside chimney and the front vestibule will simplify the heating problem. The first-floor level is above the ordinary height of packed snow in winter, but the grade entrance gives easy communication with both the cellar and the main part of the house. This permits convenient use of the cellar as a wash room and laundry, if in a well-drained location, as well as for storage purposes.

The house is roomy and well arranged, with a downstairs bedroom and bathroom. By a slight change to make the second floor like the first, a bathroom or toilet could be arranged in the large closet by the stairs. Storage space is provided in the attic.

All second-floor partitions are directly above those of the first floor, thus making a strong, rigid house with the least framing material.

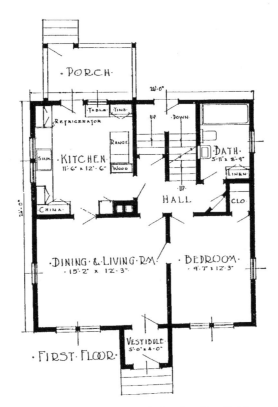

[32] Prepared by H. W. Orth and R. A. Gmeinder for the division of agricultural engineering, University of Minnesota.

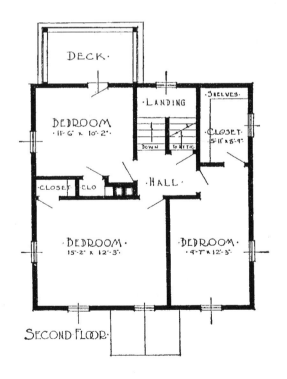

DECK·

LANDING

·SHELVES·

BEDROOM
·11'-6" x 10'-2"·

CLOSET·
·5'-1" x 8'-9"·

DOWN   TO ATTIC

·CLOSET· CLO   ·HALL·

BEDROOM·
·15'-2" x 12'-3"·

BEDROOM·
·9'-7" x 12'-3"·

·SECOND FLOOR·

VERY SMALL HOUSES

The dimensions of the houses in the very-small-house group are kept to the minimum by using the living rooms for sleeping rooms at night. These houses cannot be considered adequate for the typical farm family, but will serve for young married couples or for tenants with small families.

PLAN 6501 [33]

Floor areas: Superstructure, 325 square feet. Stoop, 15 square feet.

In plan 6501, sleeping space is provided in double-deck beds screened from the living room by draw curtains. If more space is wanted later, a bedroom wing can be added at the end of the living room. To save space, the kitchen is planned for an oil, gas, or electric stove. With a house of this size, part of the housework would have to be done outdoors, and a paved or graveled space under a tree near the house would be a convenience.

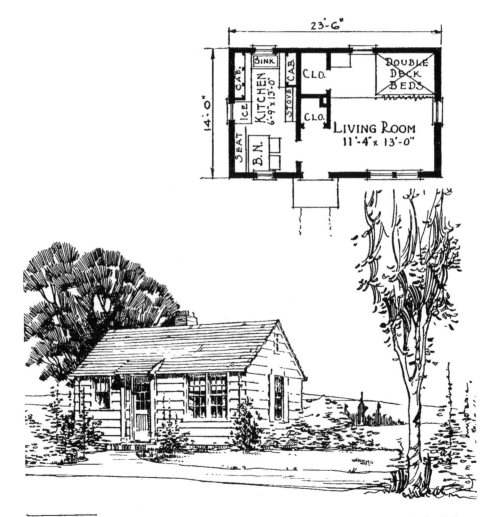

[33] Prepared by H. E. Wichers, N. F. Resch, and O. S. Ekdahl, for Kansas State College.

PLAN 6502 [34]

Floor areas: Superstructure, 600 square feet.   Stoop, 35 square feet.

The special feature of plan 6502 is the well-arranged kitchen, with good storage space and a compact work area at one side of the direct line of travel from the back door. Some privacy at night is afforded by the double wardrobes and folding screen between the two beds in the living room. The side porch will serve the double purpose of workroom and sleeping porch. It should be screened and have curtains to keep out the rain. By adding 4 feet to the living room and an additional partition, a third room could be provided. A shower bath may be installed in the large closet as shown.

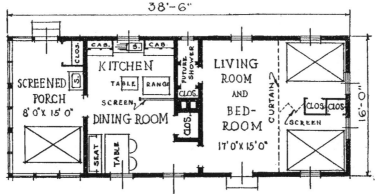

[34] Prepared by A. L. Matthews and N. G. Napier for the department of agricultural engineering, University of Arkansas.

PLAN 6503 [35]

Floor areas: Superstructure, original house 520 square feet; with addition, 825 square feet.

Small homes are often cut up into several rooms, with the result that in them a person has a "boxed-in" feeling. In plan 6503 the rooms are few, and each is used for more than one purpose. If the cost must be kept to a minimum, the bedroom and sleeping porch may be omitted in the original construction. The kitchen-dining room is unusually large for a house of this size, and the equipment is grouped in the front part of the room where the housewife can have a good view of the highway.

When the bedroom and sleeping porch are built, the bunk in the kitchen-dining room may be taken out to provide more dining space; or if one desires a cellar under part of the house, the cellar stairway may replace the bunk space. A large window and high-beamed ceiling are features of the living room. The chimney must not be too small; it is a feature of the house.

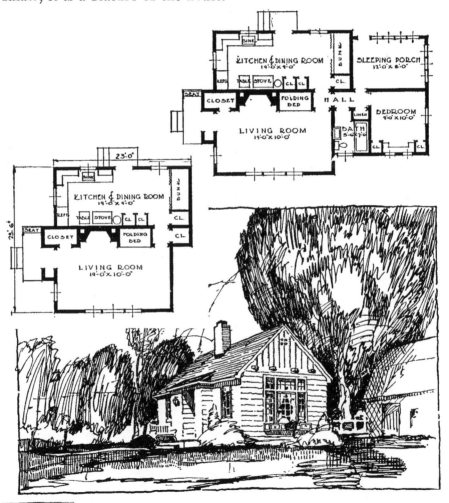

[35] Prepared by R. A. Deal and W. W. DeNeff for the department of agricultural engineering, State College of Washington.

PLAN 6504,[30] FOR THE SOUTHWEST

Floor areas: Superstructure, 430 square feet. Porches, 145 square feet.

Plans 6504 and 6505 were designed for the central valleys of California, where outdoor sleeping is invited by the mild nights.

These were designed for temporary homes to be used later as shops, bunk houses, storage buildings, or for other uses, so concrete floors are recommended. Low-cost "frameless" construction is shown in the working drawings. There are no ceilings. The shower baths shown in the plans can be installed cheaply.

The kitchens and work porches are large enough for the needs of a good-sized family. Plenty of windows are provided for ventilation. The kitchen arrangement shows a wood-burning stove, and a large refrigerator placed against an inside wall for protection from the outdoor heat. It is expected that meals will ordinarily be eaten in the kitchen or outdoors.

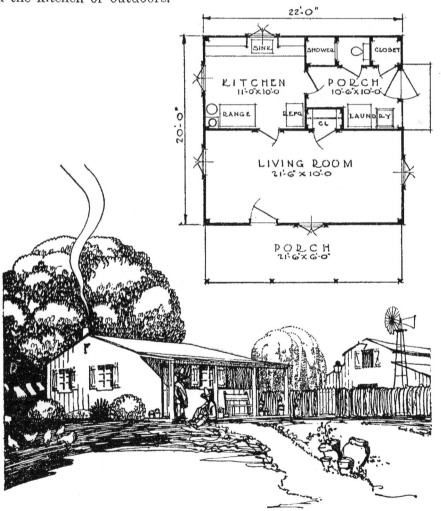

---

[30] Prepared by W. K. Bartges and Earl Barnett for the department of agricultural engineering, University of California.

PLAN 6505,[36] FOR THE SOUTHWEST

Floor areas: Superstructure, 410 square feet. Porches, 125 square feet.

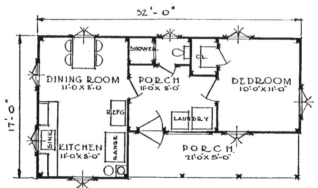

[36] Prepared by W. K. Bartges and Earl Barnett for the department of agricultural engineering, University of California.

PLAN 6506,[37] FOR NEW ENGLAND

Floor areas: Superstructure, 540 square feet. Porches, 60 square feet.

Though the rooms in plan 6506 have been kept as small as possible in order to reduce cost, good use of space is realized in the arrangement. Additions to the house would enable it to accommodate an average-sized family.

A work-porch addition beside the kitchen and living room, between the windows, would provide a place for laundry work and for hanging outer wraps. A bathroom might be built by enclosing a portion of the front porch and enlarging the window to make a doorway from the hall. If desired, a third bedroom could be added at the end of the living room.

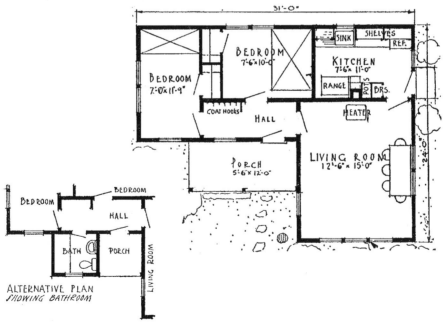

[37] Prepared by Bernhard Dirks for the department of agricultural engineering, Massachusetts State College.

PLAN 6507,[38] FOR THE NORTH

Floor areas: Superstructure, original house, 380 square feet; with first addition 600 square feet. Porches and entrances, 50 square feet. Cellar, first unit 380 square feet; with addition 600 square feet.

Plan 6507 is intended for snowy sections, and the first floor is purposely raised above the winter snow level. The house can be built in either one or two stages.

No partition divides the kitchen and living room, which permits heating the house with the kitchen range in mild weather. It also aids ventilation in summer and facilitates serving of meals in the living room.

The steps to the cellar are outside the house, protected by a storm door. There is ample space in the cellar for laundry and storage. A cistern under the kitchen provides soft water.

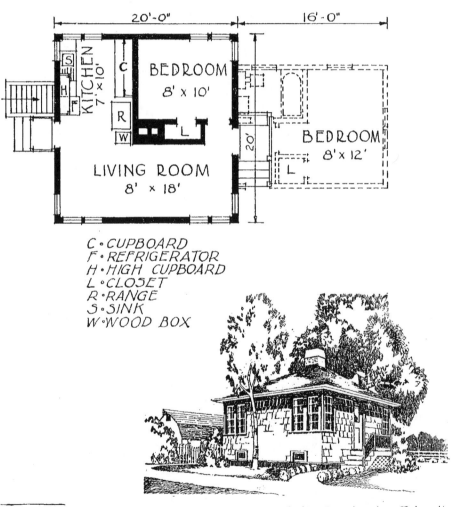

C · CUPBOARD
F · REFRIGERATOR
H · HIGH CUPBOARD
L · CLOSET
R · RANGE
S · SINK
W · WOOD BOX

[38] Prepared by S. A. Witzel for the department of agricultural engineering, University of Wisconsin.

PLAN 6508,[39] FOR THE NORTHWEST

Floor areas: Superstructure, first stage 385 square feet; second stage 605 square feet; third stage 755 square feet. Porches and steps, first stage 20 square feet; second and third stages 70 square feet.

This house is designed for the minimum requirements of beginners on the land, the first portion being 16 by 24 feet outside. It may either be enlarged for a permanent dwelling or later used as a service building. The bedroom is ample in size, but the living room, because it must also be used temporarily as a kitchen and dining room, will be crowded. This unit may be made 18 feet instead of 16 feet wide. Later the kitchen and a small bedroom may be added at the rear of the first unit, with a side porch off the kitchen. The door between the kitchen and living room will then be changed to the right of the chimney, and a narrow hall taken off the rear of the front bedroom.

If an additional bedroom is desired, it can be added to the left of the bathroom, making the third stage for this house. The closet in the kitchen should be removed and a door cut through to allow easy access from the kitchen to the bath and bedrooms. The bedroom closets must be rearranged to allow for these changes.

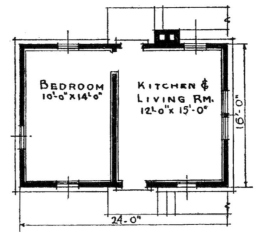

[39] Prepared by R. A. Deal and W. W. DeNeff for the department of agricultural engineering, State College of Washington.

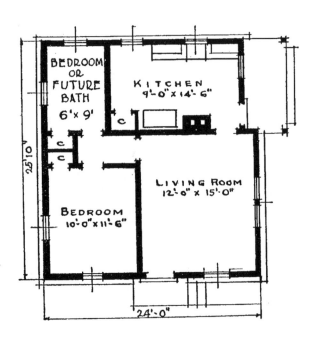

PLAN 6509,[40] FOR THE SOUTH

Floor areas: Superstructure, 525 square feet. Porches and steps, 90 square feet.

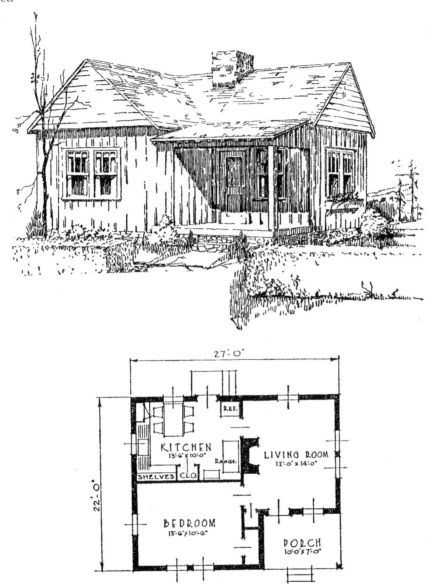

Plans 6509 and 6510, for the South and the Middle West, respectively, are low-cost houses for families that need only one bedroom. The kitchens are well arranged and have good storage space. Closet space also is ample for houses of this size.

A storage and work room, as shown in plan 6510, is a good feature for the North but is not so much needed in the South, where mild

[40] Prepared by W. C. Breithaupt and H. W. Dearing for the department of agricultural engineering, Alabama Polytechnic Institute.

PLAN 6510,[41] FOR THE MIDDLE WEST

Floor areas: Superstructure, 740 square feet. Porches and steps, 60 square feet.

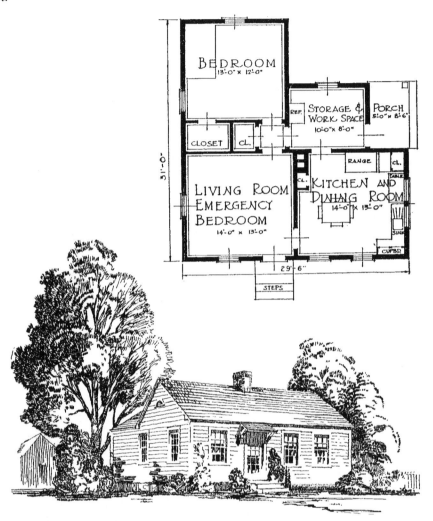

weather permits doing much housework outdoors. The living-room fireplace and kitchen range should heat house 6509 comfortably under ordinary southern conditions, but in the North arrangements should be made for a stove or circulator heater as in plan 6510.

[41] Prepared by H. J. McKee and Arthur Wupper for the department of agricultural engineering, University of Illinois.

Front porch of Clark home built by FSA (Farm Security Administration). Coffee County, Alabama, photo by John Collier, 1941   See Design 6517

Prosperity Plans Today

A decade-long home building boom came to a crashing halt in 2008. Financial shenanigans by mortgage brokers, bankers, Wall Streeters and home buyers caused a worldwide credit crisis unlike any since the Great Depression.

During the boom, just about everyone wanted a big-volume McMansion. It wasn't good to build less than five bedrooms or fewer than three parking spaces in the garage. It wasn't good to have ceilings that were less than ten feet high. Dens and kitchens had to be huge enough to startle friends and neighbors.

And, why not? Money was cheap and available everywhere. If you missed all of the daily calls from mortgage brokers, you could just fill out an application online and be approved in minutes. Why not build too much? Every penny put into a home would be paid back by inflation year in and year out. Right?

Well, those ideas didn't work out for a lot of home builders. Some people started to think that it might not be good to pay the heating, cooling and tax bills on those boom-time behemoths.

In the past, when other periods of exuberant home building came to an end, house styles changed. The elaborate Queen Anne Victorian houses of the Gay Nineties and the enormous Beaux-Arts mansions of the Roaring Twenties lost in popularity to smaller homes and simpler styles.

This time it will probably be the same. Multi-gabled mini mansions have had their run, but it's probably over now. Some other type of home will replace them in the dreams of people who are planning to build. Whatever those new homes look like, they will probably be more sensible, more efficient and less expensive.

New books, blogs and websites are extolling the virtues of tiny houses. Those may be the new wave. They make a lot of sense. The simplest way to save on home construction cost, on the expense of heating and cooling a home and on the torture from the tax collector is to build the smallest house that a family or a single homeowner can be comfortable in.

One trick is to figure out just how small that is. The other is to make sure that the family doesn't change, and that the homeowner stays single.

But, the reality is that families do change. With births, deaths, aging, marriages, friendships, divorces and all of the other circumstances of life, a family is never the same from one year to the next.

Homes should be built to last for generations. To do that, they need to adapt to their owners' needs. They need to change as a family changes. That's easy with a big house – just close the door of a room that's not needed or switch a den into a bedroom or office. It's not so easy with a small house. Those can only be truly adaptable if they can be expanded gracefully.

That's why the lessons in the designs of the Growing Houses in this book are so valuable today. Any architect, designer or home builder who is creating a new small house should think about how that house could be changed over the years. Anyone who is convinced that small or downright tiny homes are the wave of the future has to think about the wave that comes after that.

The Growing Houses were carefully planned to look good and to work well for their families in each of their stages. Two or three different stages were designed as logical progressions. Additions could be made with very little disruptions to the existing homes and to family life.

Growing Houses gave people options. They let families spread the cost of construction out over the years. The designs let them help create the perfect home for their current needs. The designs also let them change that home as those needs changed.

It really isn't that difficult to design a home that can grow. It just takes logical decisions and arranging rooms and hallways around a small core of necessary spaces and utilities. It requires that designers think about the last stage first and work backwards a bit. Anyone who studies the plans in this book can see how it's done.

To think of it, each design of a growing house gives its architect the opportunity to design two or three great houses at the same time. That's pretty exciting for anyone who loves to create.

If you're dreaming of a home that you can't quite afford right now, you might get some inspiration from the Growing Houses too. Why wait forever? Why not build something that you can afford? A little home that's designed to grow with your family could be the first step to your dream.

About the Working Drawings

The U.S. Department of Agriculture program that produced the farmhouse plans in this book continues today as the Cooperative Farm Building Plan Exchange. Still centered in the agricultural and agricultural engineering departments of state universities, the program continues to make the old plans available today.

The construction drawings of most of the homes in Farmers' Bulletin #1738 have been scanned by the North Dakota State University Extension Service and are available for you to download for free. The small-scale digital prints are direct reproductions of the original blueprints that were created in 1934. They have not been updated for modern use.

The drawings, like the floor plans in this book, should be used for conceptual purposes only. They do not replace the need for competent professional design assistance in developing safe, legal, useful, durable and attractive homes. Layouts, room dimensions, details and construction methods shown on the 1934 drawings do not meet modern construction standards and don't meet current building code requirements.

Internet Resources

Visit www.ProsperityPlans.net for quick links to free downloadable prints of the original, 1934 working drawings for most of the farmhouses presented in USDA Farmers' Bulletin #1738.

You'll also find direct links to other Cooperative Farm Building Plan Exchange archives with free downloadable plans for other farmhouses, cabins, cottages, barns and outbuildings, and online editions of other USDA Farmers' Bulletins.

Farmhouse. Coalins Forest and Game Reservation, between Tennessee and Cumberland Rivers in Kentucky, photo by Carl Mydans, 1936

Penderlea Homesteads, NC, photo by Arthur Rothstein, 1937   See Design 6514, Reversed

Made in the USA
Charleston, SC
26 April 2010